Messing with Justice

MESSING WITH JUSTICE
Ecuador: Justice Under Goverment Control

Andrés Páez

InterAmerican Institute for Democracy
Publishing Fund
Miami, 2014

ISBN: 978-1497559660

Library of Congress Catalog Number: 2014937838

Design and Cover by: Alexandria Library, Miami

Traductor: Nelson Durán

First Spanish Edition
By Paradiso Editores
Quito, Ecuador
paradiso@uio.satnet.net

The Interamerican Institute for
Democracy is a non-governmental,
nonprofit organization created to
promote and support liberty, democracy
and institutionalism in Latin America.

InterAmerican Institute for Democracy
2600 Douglas Rd, Suite 906,
Miami, FL 33134, U.S.A.
www.intdemocratic.org
Email: IID@intdemocratic.org

For my children, Andrés Felipe and Analía Milagros, the shining light of my life

Table of contents

EXHIBITS

Introduction

When and how, an elected government loses its democratic legitimacy? This process of distortion of democracy can occur in stages, along with the disappearance of the fundamental elements that constitute a representative democracy, elements well defined by the Inter-American Democratic Charter.

All of them are essential. But if I had to give priority to one of them, the fundamental requirement is the independence of the judiciary, with any doubt.

With capable, honest and irremovable judges, citizens are guaranteed in their rights. With an independent justice, Rafael Correa would not be, as his is, a threat to press freedom, his obsessive goal.

The delegitimation democratic process has been persistent in Ecuador, and its turning point has been "*la metida de mano en la justicia*" (poking hand in justice)." This process is thoroughly described by Andrés Páez in this book, which was identical to that process developed in Venezuela, Nicaragua and Bolivia, and also tried, unsuccessfully, by Cristina Kirchner in Argentina, under its project of "democratization of justice."

In this long process, under the so-called "citizens' revolution ", Rafael Correa has deleted all the characteristics of a republican system institutions, and as Paez says, the last space that had not yet established was that of justice.

It is precisely to control this justice that the Ecuadorian president, proposed to modify it, in order to improve the courts. According to his particular vision, "poking hands in justice."

Allowing better understanding of the intentions of the "storyteller of Carondelet," (as Nicolas Marquez called him) , we need to observe that his proposal is not new . It repeats the same call of the 21th century socialism other governments, and tend to undermine individual rights, remain in power and achieve impunity procedures.

We are witnessing the configuration of the dictatorships of the 21th Century, as rightly described by Osvaldo Hurtado and Carlos Sánchez Berzaín, among others, that contrary to traditional military coups now attack the democratic system itself, from inside.

There is no external debate about democracy and its legitimacy. Nobody today would try an alternative system with some probability of success. As stated by Sartori, democracy has no opposition in sight, because even authoritarian governments are sheltered under the cloak of some elementary form of democracy.

Nevertheless, a group of nominal democracies have slid into authoritarian regimes, but without the rights and institutions that are fundamental to the functioning of a democratic system. One reason why experiments fail is that they rely only on the elections and do not value the other elements of democracy. Based only on an electoral majority (real or hypothetical) this type of government try to consider itself a democracy. But as Dahl explains, no one has ever argued that democracy can or should do what majorities want, and nobody -except their enemies-

defines democracy in that way. All pro-democracy defi-
nitions involve the idea that the majority should be subject to limitations. That is the essence of democracy, that
Correa ignores.

From a theoretical point of view is possible and logical
to propose a system of government where the majority has
no limitations. What is impossible to hold is that this kind
of government can be considered a democracy.

In this struggle between democracy and dictatorship,
even in disguise, we welcome this book.

Andrés Páez, a social-democrat with a long tradition,
offers a detailed, accurate and documented description
on the attempt to subjugate the judiciary to the will of the
president, in order to complete the assault to power. An
absolute power, which allows Correa to pursue his critics,
to silence the press and to ensure impunity for corruption.

One of the difficulties that the struggle for institutions
in Latin America faces is the lack of understanding by the
English-speaking world of the forms that this steady ero-
sion of democracy in the region takes place.

This was the reason why the Inter American Institute
for Democracy decided to make this translation of Paez
book, with the hope of reaching the academic and political
world.

Guillermo Lousteau

Preamble

With the coming of the "citizen revolution" government, everything appears to have been turned topsy-turvy in Ecuador. What yesterday was evil, today, seen from the revolutionary standpoint, is good. Yesterday, the wheeling and dealing ways of the old Congress were loudly denounced. Today, Ecuador has a National Assembly controlled from Carondelet Palace[1] where the old and truculent practices of yesteryear have been exponentially magnified. If in the past the politicization of the Supreme Electoral Court was rightly criticized, today, under *correísmo*, the National Electoral Council unashamedly flies the colors of Alianza PAIS, the government's political arm. The Office of the Attorney General of the Republic, the Offices of the Superintendents, all regulatory agencies, are under the thumb of Rafael Correa's government.

The last space the "citizen revolution" appeared not to have yet invaded was the justice system. Controlling it would mean taking over the country. A State the justice system of which takes its cue from the existing political order cannot but persecute its critics. And that is precisely what is now taking place.

---

1. Carondelet Palace, in downtown Quito, is the official residence of the president of Ecuador.

Rafael Correa's word is an order judges unquestioningly obey. The country watched as National Police Colonel César Carrión was sent to prison for saying that there had been no attempt to kill Correa on September 30 and having given the presidential security detail the key to flee the Quito Regiment headquarters in the midst of very serious disturbances. Imprisoned too was a group of young people from Luluncoto charged with crimes against State security; two of them remain behind bars. Riding roughshod over constitutional principles, attempts have been made to jail legislators like Enrique Herrería and Galo Lara. Assembly Member Kléber Jiménez was prosecuted without the required authorization from the National Assembly. Meanwhile, cases such as that of presidential first cousin Pedro Delgado, who was allowed to leave the country unmolested after publicly having admitted committing a crime, continue to occur without any signs of contrition or even embarrassment on the part of the government.

This book is a chronological narration of the facts and the actors in the tragicomedy that is *correísmo*. But, most of all, it aims to expose the lengths the Correa government has gone to in order to bring to heel the courts and tribunals of Ecuador.

"Messing with justice" is the last link in this chain. Correísmo has gradually taken everything over. This metastasis —as a *correísta* nominee unwittingly termed it— began on January 15, 2007, when Correa announced his decision to convene a Constituent Assembly endowed with full powers, ignoring the Legislative Branch and abusing his powers. In Montecristi, he and his minions dissolved Congress, and dozens of laws, passed with the support and the silence of a full complement of Carondelet Palace creatures, transformed the president into a legal juggernaut as society, anxious for a change in the country, bemusedly watched.

Not all responsibility for this sad state of affairs can be laid at *correísmo*'s door, however. It has not invented anything. Indeed, political power has consistently tried to interfere with the judicial system throughout Ecuador's history. But time has seen to it that those who succeeded in momentarily kidnapping justice have eventually had their just deserts.

A thorough and minute investigation has enabled me to bring to light persuasive evidence of the model of rule Rafael Correa has imposed on the country and is now seeking to apply to the justice system.

The major purpose of this book is to retrieve the historic memory of the facts which, under governments past and present, have caused the separation of powers and, above all, the independence of the Judicial Branch, to be relegated to the hollow platitudes of political speechifying and clever spin.

Andrés Páez Benálcazar

Tyranny is not only the shedding of human blood. Tyranny are unlawful acts of all kinds. Tyranny is theft, left and right. Tyranny are excessive and unnecessary taxes. Tyranny are abuses, insults, breaking and entering ... Tyranny are dungeons, leg irons, uninhabited jungles. Tyranny are aggressive brazenness , indefatigable cupidity, overweening pride, fed on the humiliation of the oppressed. Tyranny is a hundred-eyed beast, an all-seeing monster, staring up and down, ahead and behind, this way and that; a prodigious wizard discovering in the center of the earth a fugitive virtue, hiding there in its own shame.

Juan Montalvo
Las Catilinarias [The Catilinarian Speeches]

PART I

THE NEW CORREÍSTA JUSTICE

1

Messing with Justice

*[They say] the president wants to mess with the Court. Of
course we do: to improve courts no one can be happy with.
And what's so strange about that?*

Rafael Correa

Thus spoke Rafael Correa referring to the very core of his
proposal to reform the justice system. He made this remarkable statement on January 25, 2011, one week after
announcing a new referendum on a nationwide broadcast. Correa's plan entailed the creation of a transitional
body, endowed with vast powers, capable of overhauling
and transforming the judiciary in 18 months. Large sectors of the population smelled a rat, though. According to
the presidential proposal, the entity that would undertake
the task was to consist of three delegates, all from political
groups favorable or linked to *correísmo*. That was sufficient
evidence that the ultimate goal was to take over a state
function which, by its very nature, ought to be removed
from political manipulation.

Correa's angry outburst did not occur in the heat of a
political rally but during the inauguration of the Day Hospital built by the Ecuadorian Social Security Institute south
of Guayaquil. It foreshadowed the coming campaign to
implement the president's proposal. Over the next four

months, President Correa would take advantage of every official act to try to convince the people of the soundness of his initiative. This was the context in which his slogan "trust me" was created, hoping to translate support for his administration into votes.[2]

As if this were not enough, the government pressed its public relations machinery into service. An aggressive advertising campaign bombarded citizens with radio and TV commercials sponsored by different ministries. Not surprisingly, the president's image did improve, albeit only slightly, as the outmatched opposition was prevented from fighting on a level field.

Almost two years have gone by since Correa's unfortunate statement. And now the country can see for itself that, in fact, the government did mess with the courts. Evidence of this pours out periodically from the National Court, the tribunals, and the courts of Ecuador whenever a case involving the government is pending before them.

There is the USD 800,000 loan made by Cofiec Bank to Argentine citizen Gastón Duzac under rather unusual circumstances. So far, no one has been punished. Only two individuals were arrested in the case but were released eight hours after Correa pronounced them innocent. Meanwhile, the men who could be the main culprits, Pedro Delgado, the president's cousin, and Delgado's brother-in-law, Francisco Endara, have not even been investigated by the state attorney's office.

---

2. According to *Market*, a public opinion polling company, President Rafael Correa enjoyed a 43% approval rate as of January 2011. This figure is quite low when compared to his approval rate in January 2007 which, again according to *Market*, stood at 84%.

There is a long list of corrupt acts which have also remained unpunished. Chief among them are the "drug-suitcase" affair; the contracts of Fabricio Correa, the president's brother; the shady deals at the Sports Ministry, led by the "check-swallower"; the misdeeds perpetrated at the Montecristi Constituent Assembly; the hundreds of questions raised by "emergency" contracts; the ashtray-equipped SUVs turned into ambulances through Health Ministry alchemy, which earned then-Minister Caroline Chang a presidential appointment as official delegate to the Andean Health Organization, to name but a few.

But the media have been the president's favorite target. Now, with the justice system brought to heel, the government has flexed its long arm. The latest example of this executive overreach is the case involving the daily newspaper *La Hora*.

On Tuesday, November 13, 2012, the acting 20th civil judge of Pichincha, Marco Albán, ordered *La Hora* to correct allegedly erroneous information and to publicly apologize to the government. The absurdity of the judgment stems from the failure to show that the information was false. According to statements made by Francisco Vivanco, *La Hora*'s chief editor, in an interview with *Radio Democracia* the day after the judgment was handed down, the judge's decision rested solely on an official communication from the Office of the President of the Republic affirming that the information published by the newspaper was erroneous.

The information published by *La Hora* stated that the government had spent 71 million dollars in advertising during the nine-month period from January to September 2012.[3] This figure had been provided by Corporación Participación Ciudadana [Citizen Participation Corporation], a non-governmental organization which has been disseminating this type of information for years and even has agreements with the National Electoral Council in recognition of its proven efficiency in conducting this kind of monitoring.

In essence, the published report explained that 23 government agencies had run different television advertisements during the time period in question. The 71 million dollar figure had been arrived at multiplying each TV spot times the standard price set by each television station. But, according to Francisco Vivanco, the government's argument, unsupported by any evidence, was that discounts of up to 70% had been granted.

Despite doubts about the judgment, the correction and the apology to the government were published the day after the judgment was issued. The newspaper moved the court to clarify its decision, but Judge Albán denied the motion ten days later, stating that the judgment was quite clear, although he never provided any legal basis for his finding.

This case evoked memories of another iconic judgment under *correísmo*'s new system of justice.

On February 16, 2012, in its maiden opinion, the new National Court of Justice, set up under the guidance and supervision of the Transitional Council of the Judicature (Spanish initials, CJT), upheld a lower court's judgment

---

3. *La Hora*, "71 millones en propaganda ["71 million in propaganda"], October 10, 2012.

against *El Universo*. The decision under review had sentenced the directors of the Guayaquil newspaper to three years' imprisonment and levied a fine of 40 million dollars as damages to Rafael Correa for defamation resulting from the publication on February 6, 2011, of an opinion article, "No a las mentiras" ["No to lies"], signed by Emilio Palacio.

Justices Paúl Íñiguez, Wilson Merino, and Jorge Blum upheld the judgment. The first two, as will be seen later, are close to *correísmo*. In fact, Merino played a major role in my complaint against the CJT, since he (and Paúl Íñiguez as well) received a suspiciously high score in the competition that earned him his seat on the National Court of Justice.

El Universo case attracted worldwide attention, not only because of the outlandishly high fine and the severe punishment against the newspaper's editors but also because of the presumed ideological falsity perpetrated by Juan Paredes, the acting trial judge who issued the judgment. Paredes became notorious for allegedly having read and weighed the evidence on more than 5,000 pages of the record, drafted a 156-page judgment, and served it, all within less than 24 hours, a feat which, as defense counsel for the newspaper established, is patently impossible.

Moreover, this extraordinary judgment introduced the novel concept of "contributing liability" by positing that Emilio Palacio had committed a crime and *El Universo* enabled him to do so; therefore, the owners of the Guayaquil newspaper had to be punished as well. If this reasoning were to be applied to cases such as the "drug-suitcase" matter, the minister and the under secretary of foreign relations themselves would wind up in jail, as the latter signed the regulation amending the rules governing the contents of diplomatic pouches and thus made possible a crime that embarrassed the whole country. *Ditto* in the Pedro Delgado case, where contributing liability should be imputed to his cousin, the president of the republic, for having mocked the country at large by appointing him to several top positions even though he only held a high school diploma.

To further corroborate Rafael Correa's "messing with justice," a few months after having delivered himself of that remarkable judgment against *El Universo*, Judge Juan Paredes ceased to be a temporary judge and became a full-fledged member of the Second Criminal Division of the Guayas Superior Court. A similar promotion was bestowed upon Henry Morán, another temporary judge who also heard the case against *El Universo*: he was raised to the Third Division. Ostensibly, both moved up the judicial ladder as a result of a competition. But it was a procedure marred by irregularities that gave rise to grave suspicions as to its impartiality. At the closing of the competition's early stages, both men were in the two last places, but after the final phase (a brief judicial course), they were astoundingly propelled to the top two spots.

The use of stick and carrots on those who find against or for the government was evident in the case involving Colonel César Carrión, a former director of the Police Hospital, accused of an attempt on the president's life following the September 30 revolt.

After spending seven months in prison, the Fifth Criminal Guarantees Court of Pichincha, made up of judges

Hugo Sierra, Luis Fernández, and Jacqueline Pachacama, found Carrión not guilty, as the evidence submitted by the prosecutor was insufficient to convict him. The judgment was issued on May 13, 2011.

Almost one year later, on April 18, 2012, the Transitional Council of the Judicature removed all three judges from the bench for a "most serious disciplinary infraction." The argument was that Justice Minister Johanna Pesántez had filed a grievance against them alleging that, after having acquitted Colonel Carrión, they were duty bound to order the state attorney's office to initiate new legal actions against him under criminal statutes that could be applied to the crime he had allegedly committed. The message was loud and clear: any judge who fails to toe the government line will be removed from the bench by the CJT, all three members of which are avowed *correeístas*.

2

The failed million-dollar plan

The justice system has always been in the Correa government's cross-hairs. But its first plan to restructure it seemed to wish to follow a professional approach. Plans were drawn up to purge and reform the judiciary, and an entity was hired that, at least on paper, seemed qualified for the job.

On November 17, the Justice, Human Rights, and Worship Ministry signed an agreement with the University of Talca (Chile) to conduct an audit of the Ecuadorian judicial system at a cost of one million dollars.

The university was coming to Ecuador after having completed several studies of the Chilean judicial system. Its audit was to be concluded within six months and was expected to provide the government with the tools necessary for a professional overhaul of the judiciary. It was a fully apolitical process, radically different from the work done by the Transitional Council of the Judicature.

As its report states, the University of Talca found a collapsed justice system that failed to meet even minimum efficiency requirements.

Shortcomings were brought to light in every province and canton of the country. The sluggishness of the system was the major problem the Chilean academics found. All Ecuadorians had long suspected it, but it was now evidenced by empirically verifiable parameters. The good news was that a deficiency that can be measured can also be corrected.

The study was a tool for judicial reform, as it was able to pinpoint where the government was failing in administering justice. It was now possible to know how many judges were required in each province or canton, how many courts and of what kind were necessary in the 24 provinces of Ecuador. The audit also determined the levels of proficiency required of those charged with administering justice and where those levels needed improvements. The Chilean study was clearly a valuable tool for a serious, professional reform of the Judicial Branch.

But its practical application was put on the back burner thanks to the "messing with the courts," as Corrrea candidly and correctly termed the restructuring process.

Towards a monopoly of the justice system
The first step towards a monopoly of the justice system was resolutely taken on May 7, 2011, the date of the referendum and popular consultation called by the Correa government. Ten questions were put to the citizenry; for the most part they aimed at introducing reforms in the judiciary, but also dealt with matters such as security, banking, the media, gambling, and even bullfights and cockfights.

Security was a major concern of most Ecuadorians and the hook the government used to get them to vote. Paradoxically, the lack of security was a direct result of the Correa administration's poor law enforcement record. His embrace of the notion of open borders allowed thousands of people, some of them hardened criminals, to enter Ecuador indiscriminately. These hoodlums have terrorized the country and joined the ranks of organized crime. Simultaneously, the right to bear arms was abrogated without taking into account, for instance, the realities of the rural sector. Criminal reforms, legislated by the *Congresillo* or Rump Congress, were implemented. Their questionable contents were greeted with general mirth and even indignant protests, but, on a more serious level, resulted in a spiral of crime. As a result of the judges' lackadaisical attitude — in some instances deliberate — that runs out allowable pretrial detention deadlines and precludes punishment, more than 14,000 criminals were released from jail in a demoralizing display of absolute impunity. This state of affairs was facilitated by what can only be termed a violators-release agency, the Office of the Public Defender, which from its inception was exclusively devoted the service of those who find themselves on the wrong side of the law.

This ineptness on the part of the Correa administration and the resulting increase in criminal behavior and lack of public security eventually created the conditions for the citizenry to feel the need for an in-depth restructuring of the judicial system. The excessive use of measures other than pretrial detention and even other precautionary measures in criminal cases generated greater insecurity in the country. The situation grew worse following government measures such as pardoning — by the Constituent Assembly it controlled — convicts found guilty of trafficking in up to two kilograms of drugs. As already noted, a large portion of the blame must be laid at the door of the Office of the Public Defender. This agency, the beneficiary of government largesse, had devoted all its efforts to the defense, free of charge, of thousands of criminals, leaving their victims absolutely helpless,[4] although there certainly are far more victims than privileged perpetrators. In the final analysis, the government succeeded in setting up a system of impunity well oiled by some unscrupulous judges and prosecutors and the requisite shysters, all paid by the Ecuadorian taxpayer. In spite of this mountain of evidence, the government insisted on denying reality and its then minister of the interior, Fernando Bustamante, unabashedly declared that insecurity was a matter of "simple perception," and ordered that the faces of captured criminals not be shown so that their victims could not identify them.

Referendum questions 4 and 5, transcribed below with their respective exhibits, dealt with the proposed reform of the judicial system.[5]

4. *Do you agree with replacing the current Council of the Judicature with a Transitional Council of the Judicature made up of three members elected by the Executive Branch, the Legislative Branch, and the Transparency and Social Monitoring Branch, respectively, which within a period of 18 months, not*

---

4. I introduced a bill in the National Assembly to create the Office of Defender of Crime Victims as an agency of the Office of the Attorney General. Government congressmen submitted a report during the initial consideration of the bill, challenging its legal basis, but the opposition's reaction prevented this effort to favor criminals at the expense of their victims from prospering.

5. The ten questions in the referendum and popular consultation was published in Registro Oficial No. 490 of Wednesday, July 13, 2011.

subject to extension, will exercise the functions of the Council of the Judicature and restructure the Judicial Branch, as established in Exhibit 4?

EXHIBIT 4

Article 20 of the Transitional System shall read:

"The current Council of the Judicature is hereby dissolved. To replace it, a Transitional Council of the Judicature is created, consisting of three designated delegates and their respective alternates: one each by the President of the Republic, the Legislative Branch, and the Transparency and Social Monitoring Branch; all delegates and their alternates shall be subject to impeachment. This Transitional Council of the Judicature shall have all of the powers established in the Constitution and in the Organic Code of the Judicial Branch, and shall perform their functions for a period of 18 months, not subject to extension.

The final Council of the Judicature shall be created in accordance with the procedure established in the amended Constitution. The Citizen Participation and Social Monitoring Council shall ensure that the members of the new Council of the Judicature be designated before the expiration of the Transitional Council of the Legislature's 18-month term.

The competition on the basis of qualifications being conducted by the Citizen Participation and Social Monitoring Council for the designation of the new members of the Council of the Judicature is rendered without effect.

Let the first transitional provision of the Organic Code of the Judicial Branch be deleted."

5. Do you agree with modifying the makeup of the Council of the Judicature by amending the Constitution and re-

forming the Organic Code of the Judicial Branch as established in Exhibit 5?

EXHIBIT 5

The Constitution of the Republic of Ecuador is amended as follows:

"Article 179. The Council of the Judicature shall consist of five delegates and their respective alternates, who shall be elected from lists of three candidates each submitted by the Chief Justice of the National Court of Justice, who shall preside over it; the Attorney General of the State; the Public Defender; the Executive Branch; and the National Assembly.

The delegates mentioned in the previous paragraph shall be elected by the Citizen Participation and Social Monitoring Council through a public scrutiny process with monitoring and subject to challenge by citizens.

The procedure, deadlines, and all other elements of the process shall be determined by the Citizen Participation and Social Monitoring Council.

Members and alternates of the Council of the Judicature shall hold office for six years.

The Council of the Judicature shall submit its annual report to the National Assembly, which may monitor and try the members of the former."

These two questions raised many eyebrows, as former president Osvaldo Hurtado recalls in his latest book, *Dictaduras del siglo XXI: el caso ecuatoriano* [21st Century Dictatorships: the Ecuadorian Case], published in 2012. According to President Hurtado: "The unconstitutional features of the call for a referendum were no less grave. Under the first paragraph of Article 441 of the Constitution, no constitutional amendment could be entertained that entailed a change 'in the character and constituent elements of the state, alters the fundamental structure of the Constitution, and establishes restrictions upon rights and guarantees.'"

President Hurtado underscores that the president ignored this prohibition by proposing to replace the Council of the Judicature with a Transitional Council of the Judicature made up of delegates of the president of the Republic, the National Assembly, and the Transparency and Social Monitoring Branch.

As regards Question 5, President Hurtado states that it ought to have been taken up first by the National Assembly and, once approved, submitted to the country in a referendum.

This question was significant for the "citizen revolution" scheme as it reduced the number of members of the Council of the Judicature and their sources of origin. Henceforth they would be delegates of the president of the republic, the National Assembly, and the People's Defender.[6]

However, after a campaign fought on a field sharply tilted in favor of the government — where the National Electoral Council, in an unprecedented move, declared the president to be a "political person" (the only physical person so declared), thus enabling him to travel the length and width of the country using public resources— and against those of us who opposed this storming of the judiciary by Correa, voters, by a narrow margin (52.66% to 47.34%), approved the initiative to reform the justice system.

---

6. Osvaldo Hurtado, *Dictaduras del siglo XXI: el caso ecuatoriano*, Quito, Paradiso Editores, first edition, 2012, pp. 51-52

Question 4 was also approved by an equally narrow margin (52.02% to 47.98%).

Once these results became official, the first concrete step to implement Rafael Correa's proposal to reform the justice system as he saw fit was the appointment of the three members of the Transitional Council of the Judicature charged with accomplishing this ostensible transformation in 18 months. The transformation did indeed occur, but it only entailed a change in personnel to make it more pliant to the new owners of the justice system.

As contemplated in Question 4, the Executive, Legislative, and Transparency and Social Monitoring branches of government, all controlled by Correa, were to designate their representatives to the transitional entity just created. In the end, three fervent *correístas* were chosen as members of the CJT.

Green Shirts in the Justice System
Paulo Rodríguez was the designated representative of the Executive Branch; Fernando Yávar was chosen by the Transparency and Social Monitoring Branch; and Tania Arias represented the Legislative Branch. At its first meeting, the Transitional Council of the Judicature designated Rodríguez as its chairman. Mauricio Jaramillo,[7] who has since become a key man in this *correísta* judicial machinery, was appointed director general.

---

7. Jaramillo was an officer of the Council of the Judicature but had been seconded to the Office of the Legal Counsel to the Office of the President, headed by Alexis Mera. He was, therefore, the umbilical cord linking the CJT to the Executive Branch.

It was clear from the outset that the members of the brand new Council shared a common and quite recent *correísta* past, a circumstance that cast serious doubts on its independence, especially in view of the absolute powers it had been given over the Judicial Branch. We shall now take a closer look at the résumé of each of these new officials.

Héctor Paulo Rodríguez Molina was born in Brazil while his parents were living there, according to the curriculum vitæ of the chairman of the Transitional Council of the Judicature posted on the CJT's webpage. The same source states that at age 14, Rodríguez entered the Ecuador Military Academy "where he learned discipline, order, and perseverance." Although rather brief —barely eight lines long—, the biography highlights his command of four languages (Spanish, English, Portuguese, and German) and his stint as director of the Civil Registry which, according to him, he made into "a model of change."

The head of the Civil Registry was not the only position Rodríguez had held during the Correa administration. In fact, he had other jobs under Correa and even served one of the governments during what Correa likes to call "the rule of the parties." An article published in *El Universo* on May 18, 2011, brings out in sharper relief the profile of the current chairman of the Transitional Council of the Judicature:

> Rodriguez attained that position (director of the Civil Registry) on the strength of the recommendation of the present Minister of Industries, Verónica Sión, with whom he had worked at the National Competitiveness Council (CNPC) for over three years.

Sión had become director of the CNPC in early 2005, following Joyce Higgins's resignation. Rodríguez, who had been an advisor to the businesswoman, stayed on at the CNPC.

When Correa became president, he initially ratified Sión in her position. In 2008, when he appointed her Minister of Tourism, Rodríguez became the head of the CNPC, which was merged with the Ministry of Production.

Eduardo Egas, a director of Corpei, the agency formerly charged with promoting exports, recalls the now chairman of the CJT as a highly knowledgeable professional, responsible and committed

He —together with Sión— is credited with introducing the concept of competitiveness in Ecuador and preparing the first assessments of domestic companies in terms of their competitive standing.

'His reports provided signposts for what the country would need to do in order to reduce red tape and shorten the process for incorporating businesses,' says Egas.

However, Congresswoman Betty Amores (formerly of PAIS) observes that his links to Joyce Higgins 'make his independence rather doubtful.'

His appointment, and that of Johanna Pesántez (close to the Social Christian Party or PSC) as Minister of Justice, 'are signs of the rightward drift of the Correa administration.'

Before joining the CNPC, Rodríguez had been international relations manager at the National Telecommunications Council (Conatel) during the administration of President Gustavo Noboa.

José Pilaggi, the then-president of Conatel, describes Rodríguez as 'someone who relates very well to people.'

Rodríguez did not do technical work at the time; his duties were to establish links with international telecommunications entities.

Ulpiano Salazar, a member of the current Council of the Judicature, does not doubt Rodríguez's expertise in business administration and information technology, but points out that 'a professional lawyer has greater in-depth knowledge of the work done by administrators of justice and would be able to make better decisions ...'"

This was the profile that so captivated Rafael Correa that he named Rodríguez his representative in the Transitional Council of the Judicature. The head of state did not mind that Rodríguez professed ignorance of the law, as his engineering degree, earned at the National Polytechnic School and recorded at Senescyt on June 9, 2009, is in electronics and telecommunications.

According to the government's narrative, Rodríguez had a very successful tenure as head of the Civil Registry. His major achievements include the modernization of the Registry's infrastructure and the streamlining of the processes for retrieving documents, two improvements that, again according to the official talking points, have significantly improved customer service. Rodríguez himself has said in statements made to *Ecuadorinmediato*, a virtual newspaper,[8] on August 11, 2011, that "we did in 110 days

---

8. Ecuadorinmediato http://www.ecuadorinmediato. com/index.php?module=Noticias&func=mews_user_

what had not been done in 110 years," emphasizing his success in changing the look of an institution created in 1900 by President Eloy Alfaro, a liberal icon.

The fact is, however, that the electronics and telecommunications engineer spent a lot longer than 110 days as head of the Civil Registry. In reality, he assumed his post on August 6, 2009, and left it in mid-July 2011 to accept Rafael Correa's charge to be a member of the just-created Transitional Council of the Judicature.

Rodríguez affirmed that he transformed the Public Registry during those two years. But the change appears to have benefitted only the buildings — some of which are indeed new while many others have been refurbished, all with the taxes paid by Ecuadorians.

The Civil Registry is the entity charged with "the integral identification of all inhabitants of Ecuador, registering their civil acts, issuing secure and reliable documents, and guaranteeing the appropriate custody and handling of information," according to its institutional mission, available on the Registry's webpage.

But an investigative report published in the November 2012 issue of *Vanguardia* magazine (No. 365), shows that the Civil Registry's mission is far from being accomplished and that failures continue to plague its databases.

For instance, as far as the Civil Registry is concerned, Arturo Jarrín Jarrín, the former leader of the *Alfaro Vive*

---

view&id=155612&umt=paulo_rodriguez_dice_que_en_registro_civil_se_logro_cambios_en_tiempo_corto_y_espera_mismos_resultados_para_justicia

¡Carajo! Group[9] is still alive even though he died in October 1986 and his remains were exhumed by the state attorney's office on October 25, 2012, in an attempt to establish his cause of death.

If the information on so well-known a national figure continues to be mistaken, what can be expected in the case of ordinary citizens?

But that is not the Civil Registry's sole shortcoming. According to *Vanguardia's* investigation, the databases of the government agency responsible for issuing national identity cards continue to include an unspecified number of Colombian F.A.R.C. guerrillas. The most egregious example of this is the case of Rodrigo Granda Escobar, the so-called "F.A.R.C. Foreign Minister," who has engaged in peace negotiations with the Colombian government. In 1995, this individual bought a house in the north of Quito using a fraudulent identity card the number of which, 171493523-4, still remains valid to this day.[10]

A similar case involves Cristo Rey Mariscal Peralta, a farm laborer from Juján, in the province of Guayas, whose identity was stolen to create an identity card for Ricardo Palmera, a.k.a. "Simón Trinidad," another F.A.R.C. leader serving a 60-year sentence for kidnapping in the United States. The identity card number stolen by the Colombian convict continues to be valid and is still associated with the humble Juján laborer who, apparently, was never assigned

---

9. A clandestine *left-wing* group, founded in 1982 and named after President Eloy Alfaro.

10. *Hoy*, "Como Pedro por su casa," ["As if he owned the place"] January 20, 2005

a new one and must continue to identify himself with an identity card stolen and used to commit unlawful acts.

So, if the Civil Registry was not capable of purging its own databases, what did it use the money for? Leaving aside the investment in infrastructure, there are several documents that can shed light on this question.

On October 29, 2011, *i.e.*, a little over two months after assuming office, Director Paulo Rodríguez decided to declare a state of emergency in the Civil Registry "in order to solve a critical institutional situation and duly guarantee the right to an identity of all inhabitants of Ecuador and prevent a general commotion caused by the growing insecurity in the country which includes, among other features, the undue and fraudulent use of identity documents."[11]

Under cover of this state of emergency, the entity entrusted to this electronics and telecommunications engineer was able to enter directly into all manner of contracts. Contracts worth tens of millions of dollars were concluded with a mere stroke of the pen; the resolution signed by Rodríguez allowed him to do so. And it was so done.

One of the companies hired by the Civil Registry at that time was Controles S.A., which was supposed to digitalize all files of the identity-card-issuing entity. Controles was paid USD 12,358,928 for this work under a contract signed on October 25, 2010. Controles is also the same company hired on an emergency basis by the National Electoral Council in mid-2012 to digitalize the member-

---

11. Office of the Director General of the Civil Registry, Resolution No. DGRICIC-2009-066, signed by Paulo Rodríguez Molina, director general of the Civil Registry, Identification, and Identity Cards.

ship records of the different political movements and parties in the wake of the scandal involving a massive forgery of signatures. Its work for the National Electoral Council came under heavy criticism for its slowness, negligence, and ineptness. Going by what we have already seen, its work at the Civil Registry was not the best either.

Fernando José Yávar Umpiérrez. On Friday, July 15, 2001, Fernando Yávar Umpiérrez, of Guayaquil, was designated as the Transparency and Social Monitoring Branch's delegate to the Transitional Council of the Judicature.

The designation was the result of a three- hour meeting held at the offices of Carlos Pólit, comptroller general of the republic, located in the main building of that state agency. The meeting was also attended by Bank Superintendent Pedro Solines; Companies Superintendent Soad Mansour; People's Defender Fernando Gutiérrez; and Marcela Miranda, chairperson of the Citizen Participation and Social Monitoring Council. Yávar's name was proposed by Solines,[12] and he was unanimously selected.

And so it was that Fernando Yávar Umpiérrez, a young attorney born on July 20, 1978, became a member of the CJT. His curriculum vitæ included a stint as a prosecutor in Guayas, and specialties in criminal law and indigenous justice; he was a partner in the law offices of Ycaza y Yávar.

But his record was not spotless. While a prosecutor in Guayas, the now member of the Transitional Council of the Judicature had been suspended without pay for 15 days

---

12. Solines is an enthusiastic militant of *correísmo*. He initially worked at the Office of the President of the Republic and was subsequently nominated for the office of Superintendent of Banks and Insurance.

for having allowed pretrial detention to expire in the case of Jaime William Toro Laaz, arrested on August 21, 2008, for forgery of public documents. According to the resolution sanctioning Yávar, the prosecutor had 90 days after the filing of the indictment to submit the government's pleading in the case. This Yávar failed to do even after the presiding judge, Eduardo Salazar, 10th criminal judge of Guayas, asked him six times. At the end of the pretrial detention period, the suspect moved to be released.

It bears mentioning that Fernando Yávar Umpiérrez is the son of Fernando Yávar Núñez, the current state attorney for Durán, a controversial figure who has been the subject of at least eight serious complaints. His performance has so angered the people of Guayas that on April 25, 2012, he was pelted with eggs as he entered the Provincial Court building.[13]

The Bar Association of Guayas has been the leading critic of the Durán state attorney. It disbarred him and has expressed its indignation at the failure of the CJT, of which his son is a member, to order any sanctions against him.

Three investigations are currently pending at the State Attorney's Office against Yávar Núñez.

The Bar Association of Guayas has made a compilation of several grievances filed against the father of a member of the Transitional Council of the Judicature who, nevertheless, continues to peaceably hold the office of state attorney for Durán. These grievances include the following:

---

13. Ecuadorinmediato http://www.ecuadorinmediato. com/indez.php?module=Noticias&func=news_user_ voew&id=172032&umt=lanzan_huevos_a_fernando_yavar_ nunez_en_corte_del_guayas

Tampering with the minutes of an arraignment: During his nationwide broadcast on Saturday, March 31, 2012, Rafael Correa announced that the then 32nd criminal guarantees and traffic judge of Guayas, Ricardo La Mota, had released Edison Rivera Quila who, in the course of a police operation, had been found in possession of submachine guns, rifles, pistols, an armored vehicle, and half a million dollars in jewels.

The president published La Mota's picture during his broadcast and made this dramatic exhortation: "Parents, if this man released by this judge wounds or murders a member of your family with his machine guns and other weapons, you should know that the judge who released him is also responsible." Correa added that the Transitional Council of the Judicature had already moved to suspend Judge La Mota for three months. This was done even though no official sanction had been issued against him, according to the complaint filed by Juan Vizueta, the then acting president of the Bar Association of Guayas.

A few days later, as law enforcement officers arrested Judge La Mota, he stated that he had released the criminal under pressure, "because he didn't want any problems with the Yávars." In a video, the detained judge pleaded his case: "Mr. President, I was the victim of pressures, threats, and intimidation on the part of Fernando Yávar Núñez, Fernando Yávar Umpiérrez's dad, to change the state attorney's report and drop the request for pretrial detention."

Instigation and verbal threats: During his nationwide broadcast on Saturday, March 31, 2012, Rafael Correa announced that the then 32nd criminal guarantees and traffic judge of Guayas, Ricardo La Mota, had released Edison

Rivera Quila who, in the course of a police operation, had been found in possession of submachine guns, rifles, pistols, an armored vehicle, and half a million dollars in jewels.

The president published La Mota's picture during his broadcast and made this dramatic exhortation: "Parents, if this man released by this judge wounds or murders a member of your family with his machine guns and other weapons, you should know that the judge who released him is also responsible." Correa added that the Transitional Council of the Judicature had already moved to suspend Judge La Mota for three months. This was done even though no official sanction had been issued against him, according to the complaint filed by Juan Vizuela, the then acting president of the Bar Association of Guayas.

A few days later, as law enforcement officers arrested Judge La Mota, he stated that he had released the criminal under pressure, "because he didn't want any problems with the Yávars." In a video, the detained judge pleaded his case: "Mr. President, I was the victim of pressures, threats, and intimidation on the part of Fernando Yávar Núñez, Fernando Yávar Umpiérrez's dad, to change the state attorney's report and drop the request for pretrial detention."

Forfeiture of property owned by the Ecuadorian State: On October 22, 2009, Fernando Yávar Núñez filed a special complaint for the forfeiture of property owned by the Ecuadorian State against Aland Molestina Malta, head of the First Naval Region of the Province of Guayas.[14] The complaint averred that he [Yávar Núñez] had enjoyed uninterrupted possession of a 341 [square]-meter plot of land

---

14. The complaint was filed with the 30th civil and mercantile judge of Guayas and was drafted by Attorney Gregorio López Cerezo.

in the parish of Eloy Alfaro, canton of Durán, province of Guayas:

> ...since August 7 I have been in quiet, continuous, *i.e.*, uninterrupted, peaceable, public, unequivocal possession, as owner, *i.e.*, with the faculties of lord and master, of said real property for over FIFTEEN YEARS as of the date of filing of the present complaint. Indeed, I have built on said land, with my own money, first a frame house which became obsolete with time, and later a concrete house, likewise built with my own money, which measures 4.50 meters, front, by 12 meters, long, for a total built area of 54 square meters, plus a potable water cistern to hold this liquid, essential for daily life. All of which has been done for my personal benefit ...

In his response, Antonio Pazmiño Ycaza, first regional director of the Office of the Attorney General of the Republic, refuted Yávar Núñez's claims and affirmed that the plaintiff was seeking to appropriate for himself a piece of property belonging to the Ecuadorian state:

> ... it is a well-known fact that his residence is located on plots 9 and 10, on First Avenue, in block Z-1 of the Entrerios development, in the parish of La Puntilla, canton of Samborondón, province of Guayas. Therefore, we find ourselves before a claim to unduly appropriate a property belonging to the Ecuadorian State, under the name of the Ecuadorian Navy..."

In spite of the State's arguments, at 11:15 a.m. on February 4, 2011, by which time Yávar Umpiérrez was already a member of the Transitional Council of the Judicature, Judge Gabriel Nivela, of the 30th Civil Court of Guayas, found for the plaintiff and, consequently, Yávar Núñez became the owner through forfeiture of a property that had belonged to the State.

Representatives of the Bar Association of Guayas filed a complaint to prevent this judgment from become effective and those proceedings are still pending.

Abuse of a handicapped person: On June 15, 2011, Elena Carrión Garrotiza appeared before the third commissar of the canton of Durán to report that her niece Kathya Arellano, who is physically handicapped and who had lived for several years on a small plot in the Cinco de Junio Housing Cooperative of the canton of Durán, had been threatened with being deprived of said property. According to the report, Arellano had built a wooden and bamboo home that collapsed in a rain storm. She had then erected pillars in order to rebuild her home little by little. But on Thursday, June 9, 2011, at about 4:00 p.m., the Durán commissar called on her and told her the police was going to demolish the structure, alleging that it was not contemplated under municipal regulations; Arellano was not given the right to defend herself. Worse yet, the report goes on to say, about one and half hours later Fernando Yávar Núñez arrived on the premises and said that, as state attorney for Durán, he was taking possession of the property —which he claimed had been given to him as a gift— and would raze the dwelling to take over the land. In her report, Elena Carrión asks that her niece, a handicapped and highly vulnerable person, be shown the respect due to her, and emphatically denied that Yávar Núñez is the owner of the humble plot in question.

Graft: On December 1, 2006, Francisco Freire, assistant state attorney of Guayas, appeared before the Guayas state attorney, Jorge Blum Carcelén (a future justice of the National Court) to report a possible instance of bribery. Freire claims in his report that Attorney Fernando Yávar Umpiérrez had gone to his office to ask for his telephone number at the request of Yávar's father, Fernando Yávar Núñez. He goes on to say that he later received a call from Yávar Núñez, who requested Freire's assistance in the criminal investigation for perjury being conducted against Enrique Rodas Cárdenas.

Subsequently, at 9:00 a.m. on December 1 of that same year, the defendant's son, Enrique Rodas Ron, went to Freire's office and asked him: "Did you receive the package we sent you through Mr. Yávar?" Surprised, Freire asked for clarification and was told by Rodas Ron that it was one thousand dollars his father had borrowed at Yávar Núñez's request to give to Freire in order to enlist the latter's assistance in the perjury proceedings.

As a result of this complaint, Yávar Núñez was fined 10% of his salary.

Verbal abuse: Ana del Pilar Medina Mercado, a lawyer and a resident of the canton of Durán, reported that at 2:50 p.m. on July 13, 2011, while at the offices of the state attorney for Durán, Fernando Yávar Núñez, she was verbally abused by said official. According to Medina, in the course of a deposition and as she objected to the witness' testimony, Yávar replied:

Shut up, you fool! What's the matter with you? I'm in command here, and no stupid female lawyer is going to interrupt what I'm doing." Medina immediately demanded respect as a woman and a lawyer, and, according to her, Yávar answered: "You go and complain and file a report wherever the fuck you want; I don't care. I'm in command here and I'm pissed off with this case and you [Medina] are a pain in the ass.

This grievance was filed with the then state attorney for Guayas, Antonio Gagliardo Loor, and its outcome is unknown at this time..

Tania Lizbeth Arias Manzano: Though she always denied it, the evidence speaks for itself. Attorney Tania Arias, born in Ambato on May 7, 1967, has always been closely identified with *correísmo*.

She earned her law degree at the Pontifical Catholic University of Ecuador (PUCE), where, among others, she met Fánder Falconí. When Falconí became the director of the National Planning and Development Agency (Senplades), he took her with him as a member of his work team.

As the Constituent Assembly began its deliberations in Montecristi, Arias Manzano was detailed as Senplades's delegate to advise Alianza PAIS assembly members. She played an important role in the Fundamental Rights, State Structure, and Justice and Fight against Corruption Commissions.

Her work at the Constituent Assembly was rewarded with a seat in the Election Disputes Court, whose chief judge she eventually became. Once ensconced in her new job, Arias remained silent on the uneven electoral campaign waged by Correa administration in advance of the referendum and popular consultation of May 7, 2011.

Upon a motion by the organization Mujeres por la Vida (Women for Life), a women's rights group that actively campaigned for the government at the time of the 2011 referendum, she was appointed delegate to the Transitional Council of the Judicature.

Further evidence of her identification with the government is her enthusiastic participation in the mass meeting held on Tuesday, August 11, 2009, at the Atahualpa Olympic Stadium[15] to celebrate the second anniversary of the "citizen revolution". This event was attended by the presidents of Cuba and Venezuela, Hugo Chávez and Raúl Castro, respectively. Arias, who at the time was the chief judge of the Election Disputes Court, is shown in photographs standing next to top government officials. Her active role at this *correísta* lovefest denied any possibility of impartiality on the part of the CIT.[16]

José Mauricio Jaramillo Velasteguí: At its first official meeting, the Transitional Council of the Judicature asked for the resignation of acting Director General Gustavo Donoso Mena to pave the way for the appointment of Mauricio Jaramillo Velasteguí, a lawyer born in Quito on March 19, 1974. The official government explanation was that Jaramillo's appointment recognized his efficient work as a career official in the Council of the Judicature for over 15 years.

---

15. A photograph published in the newspaper *Expreso* and showing Arias at the meeting is attached.

16. On the other hand, the author was prosecuted before the Election Disputes Court in baseless proceedings brought against him for having placed a simple placard in a friend's yard.

Although Jaramillo Velasteguí has chosen to keep a low profile, he certainly has become well versed in political matters. Earlier in his career he was seconded to work at the Office of the President of the Republic. He was a close advisor to National Legal Secretary Alexis Mera, Rafael Correa's right-hand man.

One of Jaramillo's best known acts as representative of the Executive Branch was his defense of the government's position in the action for protection of constitutional rights filed in connection with the mandatory nationwide broadcast of September 30. It should be recalled that during the police and military revolt on that day, the government suspended all broadcasts by private media and ordered them to rebroadcast the programming on the government-owned TV station *Ecuador TV*.

The action for the protection of constitutional rights was filed in mid-2010 by Assembly Members César Montúfar, Fausto Cobo, Leornardo Viteri, Fernando Aguirre, and myself. Its purpose was to determine whether the right of citizens to receive information had been violated by that mandatory nationwide broadcast. The case was decided in favor of the government by Gladys Terán, who at the time was the third criminal guarantees judge of Guayas and who today sits on the National Court of Justice.

Jaramillo Velasteguí has acted in similar proceedings on behalf of the Office of the President of the Republic. He tries to keep off newspapers, although there can be no doubt that he wields enormous power in the judicial system.

This power was evidenced by Resolution 01-CJT-DG-2011 of the Transitional Council of the Judicature, whereby Jaramillo Velasteguí, following in the steps of Paulo Rodríguez at the Public Registry, declared a state of emergency "… in order to solve the critical situation (the judiciary) is going through and duly guarantee the right of access to justice …"

Traveling under this resolution, the CJT has been able to award dozens of multimillion dollar contracts for civil and IT infrastructure, with no bidding or competition.

This state of affairs was denounced by Assembly Member Kléber Jiménez, who disclosed the existence of 39 contracts, awarded directly, with no bidding process, for the construction of an equal number of buildings throughout the country. The contracts were worth a total of USD 160,442,901.[17]

More irregular still is the circumstance that the price per square meter of construction the Council of the Judicature contracted for was significantly higher than those obtained by other entities. The average price the country pays for new buildings for the Judicial Branch is USD 966 per square meter,[18] and there are instances of other government agencies obtaining considerably lower prices.

Awarding contracts directly, without benefit of bidding and under declared emergencies, is a hallmark of this administration. The practice began under Jorge Marún when he was public works minister in 2007. His "Blitz Plan" awarded public works contracts worth millions of

---

17. Council of the Judicature, Official Communication No. 1533-DG-CJ-12-SEP, addressed to Assembly Member from the Province of Zamora Chinchipe Kléber Jiménez, July 4, 2012.

18. *El Universo*, Monday, November 19, 2012

dollars with no bidding or competition, triggering dozens of complaints.

Now, and thanks to Mauricio Jaramillo Velasteguí and with the blessings of its three members, the Transitional Council of the Judicature has implemented its own "Blitz Plan," choosing, according to published reports, companies identified with government officials and people with insufficient expertise.[19]

Correísta Justice Takes Shape

The Transitional Council of the Judicature presented its report for 2011-2012 on August 1, 2012, in the chamber of the former Senate.

Like students in an oral examination, each of the CJT members climbed the rostrum and, in the presence of government authorities and Assembly members, proceeded to list what, in his or her opinion, were the greatest achievements of the transitional entity during its first 12 months of work.

First to speak was Chairman Paulo Rodríguez, who highlighted the 193 million-dollar investment in infrastructure and IT, and the processing of thousands of cases previously held up.

Fernando Yávar and Tania Arias next emphasized the talent that had been recruited for the judiciary and would help build a new image for a shopworn Judicial Branch.

All three officials agreed that the most significant accomplishment of their tenure had been the installation

---

19. *El Universo,* "Consejo dio millonario contrato a compañía de $800 de capital" ['Council awarded a multimillion contract to a company with $800 corporate stock"], November 25, 2012

of the new National Court of Justice, made up of 21 justices selected in a competition designed and organized by themselves.

The competition began on August 24, 2011, and concluded on January 26, 2012, with the formal installation of the 21 new justices and their respective alternates in the remodeled Sucre National Theater, in downtown Quito.

The Makeup of the National Court

The process of selecting the justices for the new National Court of Justice got officially underway with the publication by the Transitional Council of the Judicature of a document awkwardly called: "Rules and regulations for the competition on qualifications, citizen challenges, and social monitoring for the selection of female and male servants of the Judicial Branch" (Exhibit 2, pag 176). This document established the framework for the competition and was published on August 24, 2011.

Of a total of 666 candidates who submitted applications, 483 were eliminated during the first round, when credentials were verified, suitability was evaluated, and psychological evaluations performed.

The candidates going on to the second round of the selection process included lawyers like Raúl Ilaquiche, married to Assembly Member Lourdes Tibán; Benjamín Cevallos, chairman of the former Council of the Judicature; Juan Falconí Puig, a former superintendent of banks; and several trial and appellate judges, most of them with years of experience on the bench. Notoriously absent from this list were justices who had served in the now abolished Supreme Court, except for Carlos Ramírez, the acting chief justice of the National Court, subsequently reelected to the post at the end of the competition.

Following initial screenings, the selection process provided for theoretical and practical evaluations of the candidates and a personal interview. This interview was given a maximum weight of 10 points. It was nothing more than a 15-minute chat between each candidate and the three members of the Transitional Council of the Judicature.

Curiously, the interviews were scheduled at the end of the process, after completion of the previous rounds, at a time when the candidates' scores were already known. It was easy, therefore, to give low grades to candidates the CJT did not wish to see as National Court justices and high grades to those it desired to promote to the highest court in the land. And that was precisely what happened. So scandalous was the CJT's behavior that the International Monitoring Commission (*Veeduría Internacional* or VI) felt duty bound to object.

The competition —such as it was— having been completed, the makeup of the new National Court of Justice was announced:

Ramírez Romero, Carlos Miguel
Bermúdez Coronel, Óscar Eduardo
Robalino Villafuerte, Vicente Tiberio
Granizo Gavidia, Alfonso Asdrúbal
Ojeda Hidalgo, Álvaro Vinicio
Suing Nagua, José
Blum Carcelén, Jorge Maximiliano
Merino Sánchez, Wilson Yovanny

Benavides Benálcazar, Merck
Andino Reinoso, Wilson Efraín
Ayluardo Salcedo, Johnny Jimmy
Íñiguez Ríos, Paúl Manuel
Merchán Larrea, María Rosa
Pérez Valencia, Maritza Tatiana
Espinoza Valdivieso, María del Carmen
Salgado Carpio, Carmen Alba del Rocío
Terán Sierra, Gladys Edilma
Aguirre Suárez, María Paula Elizabeth
Vintimilla Moscoso, María Ximena
Yumbay Yallico, Mariana
Blacio Pereira, Lucy Elena

Availing myself of my prerogatives as a member of the National Assembly, I conducted an inquiry into this selection process. After subpoenaing a large volume of information from public and private entities in a probe lasting several months, I was able to unearth serious flaws in the competition.

Using certified documentation, I established manifold violations of the legal framework. Points were awarded to candidates who had not even met the necessary requirements to qualify. Favored candidates included an obvious majority of Correa sympathizers, thus seriously affecting the impartiality that is a *sine qua non* of justice. Rodríguez and his accomplices thought they would get away with it; that no one would bother to read through hundreds of documents. But I did. Below are the results of my investigation.

The case of Mariana Yumbay Yallico

She was hailed as the first indigenous woman to be designated justice of the highest court in the land. A press release issued on February 8, 2012, by the government agency Andes[20] praised Mariana Yumbay as a 38-year old woman from Guaranda, a graduate of the local Miguel Ángel Polibio high school. According to Andes's hagiography, Yumbay's first calling had been medicine, but thanks to her uncle, Arturo Yumbay, Guaranda's first indigenous mayor, she eventually decided to become a lawyer.

"My uncle guided me, and I owe him my career and perhaps everything I am today. He taught me values, particularly pride in my identity; he taught us to honor our parents and our culture," the newly designated justice told Andes.

But one important value in indigenous culture is the rejection of lies. And lie is precisely what Yumbay did when she accepted her seat on the National Court of Justice as the result of an undeserved score in the selection process.

My investigation revealed that Yumbay's law degree was issued on March 15, 2001 (Exhibit 3. page 177) by the Central University of Ecuador. This means that at the time her candidacy was put forth, the now justice of the National Court had had exactly ten years of experience as a lawyer.

---

20. ANDES, Ecuador and South America Public News Agency, "Mariana Yumbay: una designación histórica en la justicia ecuatoriana" ["Mariana Yumbay: an historic designation in the Ecuadorian justice system"], February 8, 2012

The call, the rules and regulations, and the instructions (Exhibit 4, page 178)[21] used for the competition clearly state that a candidate had to establish a minimum ten-year experience and that for each year after those first ten, two additional points would be given. This was ignored by the Transitional Council of the Judicature as it awarded Yumbay six points as if she had had 13-year experience instead of the ten she actually had. The indigenous "justice" accepted the post without mentioning the six-point gift she had received.

As part of my investigation into the designation of justices of the new National Court of Justice, I subpoenaed Attorney Yumbay for deposition.

The deposition took place on November 6, 2012. Under an examination lasting approximately half an hour, Yumbay had to admit that, in fact, she had graduated from law school on March 15, 2001. I then suggested that she resign from the bench as a matter of decency. She has obviously failed to do so and continues to dismiss and reject any and all matters that come before her, signing orders, decrees, and even opinions without the legitimacy required to be a justice. Yumbay, barely ten years out of law school, deserved zero points, not the six a profligate Transitional Council of the Judicature saw fit to award her.

The case of Wilson Yovanny Merino Sánchez

This "justice" came under the spotlight when he wrote the opinion that upheld the judgment against *El Universo*,

---

21. Instructions for the competition on qualifications, citizen challenges, and social monitoring for the selection and designation of female and male justices of the National Court of Justice. Resolution No. 007-2011 of the National Council of the Judicature

an unprecedented three-year prison sentence against the newspaper's editors and 40 million in damages to Correa for slander.

Merino's upholding of that extraordinary judgment was in the headlines all over the world. Execution was forestalled only when the Inter-American Commission on Human Rights (IACHR) stepped in with its finding that the judgment violated basic human rights, a violation which Ecuadorian judges, Merino foremost among them, somehow had failed to notice.

Born in Santa Rosa, Province of El Oro, on September 21, 1971, Merino made his way to the high court on the strength of his record as state attorney in his home province and professor at the Technical University of Machala. According to press clippings, he was also the respondent in an alimony case filed by his former wife, Nancy Jaramillo González, and had entered the selection process for the post of People's Defender but had been disqualified for not meeting several requirements.[22]

In the first round of the selection process for the National Court, Merino scored 27.5 points (Exhibit 14), barely enough to move on to the second round.

But the documentation I examined during my investigation showed several anomalies in his score that prove this individual should never have gone beyond the first round.

The Transitional Council of the Judicature awarded Merino ten points for his additional years of experience.

---

22. *El Universo*, "Nueva Corte Nacional de Justicia se estrenó con un fallo a favor de Rafael" ["New National Court of Justice maiden opinion finds for Rafael {Correa}"], February 19, 2012

The rules established that a candidate had to have practiced law for at least ten years before submitting his application and that two extra points would be awarded for each year after those initial ten, as we have previously seen in the case involving Yumbay. In other words, the CJT considered Merino as having 15-year experience as a lawyer.

It so happens, however, that Merino's law degree was issued on March 26, 2001, by the Catholic University of Cuenca. This means that the now-justice barely met the 10-year experience requirement to enter the selection process. If the extra points he undeservedly was awarded had been taken away, Merino would not have gone beyond the first round.

And as if this were not enough, in his presentation kit the now-justice claimed to have been a free-lance lawyer since 2001. However, the Internal Revenue Service confirmed that Merino had been registered as a higher education instructor since 1993 (Exhibit 7). In other words, during the years he claimed to have been a free-lance lawyer, Merino never invoiced a client for legal services. IRS Director Carlos Marx Carrasco has not opened an investigation into this potential case of tax evasion. My requests that he do so have been to no avail, as he has simply refused to investigate the matter, in stark contrast with the diligence he usually displays in other cases.

As part of my investigation, I also subpoenaed Merino. Twice he failed to obey the subpoena and I had to move the presiding judge to order law enforcement to compel Merino to appear. Astonishingly, the judge not only denied my motion and thereby my right to compel compliance with the subpoena by law enforcement, but set a new date for the deposition, an exceptional occurrence in the judicial field. Finally, Justice Merino showed up for his deposition (Exhibit 8). Shaking, perspiring profusely, and accompanied by a bodyguard, he answered the questions put to him. He had to admit that at the time he was raised to the National Court he had barely been ten years out of law school. Consequently, he should have been awarded zero extra points, but the Transitional Council of the Judicature gave him ten, to the evident detriment of other candidates who had met that requirement. In the case of Wilson Merino, the extra ten points enabled him to clear the hurdle of the first round. For his interview or oral hearing, where he expatiated on his bizarre desire to join the National Court to bring about a "constitutional metastasis," he was awarded seven points (out of a possible ten). His opinion against *El Universo* is proof positive of his metastatic success.

Even though Merino confirmed at his deposition all the complaints against him, the Transitional Council of the Judicature has remained silent on the issue. In fact, it would seem that the National Court itself is supporting him, as he has been assigned several high-profile cases such as those involving the expropriated television channels, the proceedings against former President Abdalá Bucaram, the lawsuit brought by populist leader Edgar Coral against the president of the republic for defamation and slander, and the sports ministry case involving Fernando Moreno, a.k.a. "the check-swallower," and Raúl Carrión, a former minister and treasurer of Correa's first electoral campaign.

The case of María Ximena Vintimilla Moscoso

The case involving this lawyer, born in Cuenca on March 31, 1968, is closely related to the first two we have just seen, as it also has to do with the awarding of underserved points. And her past identifies her as someone closely tied to the present administration.

Her relationship with the government of the "citizen revolution" began at the Montecristi Constituent Assembly in 2008 when she was named advisor to her fellow Cuencan, Alianza PAIS Assembly Member Rosana Alvarado, with a monthly salary of USD 3,200.

In 2009 she became legal counsel to Fánder Falconí, who at the time was Ecuador's foreign minister (Exhibit 10). Subsequently she was appointed Under Secretary for Emigrants to the South, a position she held from October 2010 to February 2011.

Vintimilla next worked with Cuenca Mayor and Alianza PAIS member Paúl Granda as director of institutional development and human talent, earning a monthly salary of USD 3,300.

Vintimilla had received her law degree from the University of Azuay on September 18, 1998 (Exhibit 11). At the time her nomination was submitted, she had 12-year experience as a practicing lawyer and was therefore entitled to no more than four extra points during the qualifications round of the selection process.

But, once again, the Transitional Council of the Judicature inexplicably awarded Vintimilla a total of eight points. And during the final personal meeting with the judicial triumvirate, she scored 9.5, a score high enough to raise her to 16th place of a possible 21 (Exhibit 14).

She was deposed at my request and had to admit she had been a practicing lawyer for only 12 years and that, therefore, she could not deserve the eight points she had been awarded. She took advantage of her deposition to make biased remarks about my performance. I was surprised, therefore, when a few days later she texted me her telephone number and requested a meeting. Needless to say, I did not bother to reply.

In May 2012, Vintimilla was assigned the case of former President Jamil Mahuad. But defense counsel for Mahuad showed that the case had not gone through the regular assignment process as the document assigning the case to Vintimilla had not been signed by the court official in charge. Based on this irregularity, defense counsel for the former president sought to recuse Justice Vintimilla who, oddly enough, waited until December 12, when the electoral process was already underway, to issue a bench warrant for the arrest of former President Mahuad.

The case of María Augusta Sánchez Lima

This candidate excused herself from being sworn in as an associate justice when I reported that she had been unduly favored by the Transitional Council of the Judicature.

María Augusta Sánchez, born in Quito on August 8, 1974, earned her law degree at the Pontifical Catholic University of Ecuador (PUCE) on April 13, 1998 (Exhibit 13). Under the instructions for the selection process for justices of the National Court, she was entitled to two extra points. But the Transitional Council of the Judicature in its wisdom saw fit to award her six, thus allowing her to move on to the next round instead of being disqualified, as she ought to have been, on account of her low score.

The case of Lucy Elena Blacio Pereira

Born in Santa Rosa, El Oro, on June 3, 1968, Lucy Blacio was an assistant state attorney in her home province between 2003 and 2008. In 2009 she was promoted to state attorney. She resigned, according to her, because of pressure from the then attorney general of Ecuador, Washington Pesántez.

Her last position before being designated justice of the National Court of Justice was as transparency and anti-corruption secretary in the Citizen Participation and Social Monitoring Council, where her job was to process citizen complaints. It would appear that her performance left a lot to be desired, as thousands of complaints remained unattended during her tenure.

Her professional résumé highlights the kudos she received for her role in the fight against human trafficking. She seemed a promising candidate.

Her promise remained unfulfilled. Her scores in the selection process were disappointingly low. She came in 45th place, barely under the wire, in the competition on qualifications (Exhibit 14).

But her luck changed for the better in her meeting with the members of the Transitional Council of the Judicature. She was awarded 10 points (out of a possible 10), the highest of all candidates, and thus slid into 21st place, the very last spot for justices.

Blacio's remarkable and unexpected 24-point swing following her interview eliminated Yolanda Yupanqui, a woman with an impeccable curriculum vitæ, who had shown herself to be a strong candidate. At the end of the first round of the selection process, Yupanqui held 12th place.

The one-on-one meeting with the members of the CJT was also decisive for Yupanqui, as she received a score of 1.3, well below her performance during the first round. In my capacity as a member of the National Assembly, I subpoenaed the video of Blacio's interview. I observed that Fernando Yávar was the only CJT member who asked no questions of her. Coincidentally, Yávar had been designated by the Transparency and Social Monitoring Branch, which includes the Citizen Participation Council where Blacio had worked. When the scores for the final interviews were totaled, Blacio came in on 21st place and Yupanqui on 22nd, separated by a difference of 0.55% (Exhibit 14). It was evident that the entire process had been rigged to benefit Blacio (who received the highest of all second-round scores) and to exclude a candidate who had consistently shown greater knowledge and earned higher grades.

The case of Paúl Manuel Íñiguez

Íñiguez was another justice who upheld the judgment against *El Universo*. His case is similar to Lucy Blacio's.

At the end of the first round of the selection process, Íñiguez found himself on 41st place and bidding farewell to any hope of making it to the National Court. But again the meeting with the three members of the Transitional Council of the Judicature worked its magic. With an almost perfect 9.9 score as a vaulting pole, he landed on 20th place and earned his seat on the bench.

During the first round, Íñiguez had been awarded four extra points for a master's degree in IT law (Exhibit 16), in open violation of the instructions for the selection process, which read that "judicial experience, legal publications, and specialized studies shall be related to the specialty of the Division of the National Court of Justice the candidate wishes to be considered for."[23]

Justice Íñiguez's record shows close links to *correísmo*. He was an advisor to Alianza PAIS members of the Montecristi Constituent Assembly. He was later retained by pro-government legislator Vethoween Chica as an advisor. And he ran — unsuccessfully, it should be noted — on the Allianza PAIS primaries for mayor of Gualaceo.

The case of Johnny Jimmy Ayluardo Salcedo

Candidate Johnny Ayluardo ended the first round of the selection process on 37th place, far from the first 21 places reserved for the future justices of the new National Court.

But again the prodigal hand of the Transitional Council of the Judicature bestowed the gift of a nine-point score in the final one-on-one meeting and Ayluardo jumped from 37th to 19th place (Exhibit 14).

Ayluardo is a 49-yeard old Guayaquil lawyer, appointed secretary to the Office of the Guayaquil Regional Intendent, a dependency of the Office of the Superintendent of Banks and Insurance, under the Correa administration.

Other CJT gifts

There were other cases where the help given by the Transitional Council of the Judicature proved decisive. Several

---

23. Íñiguez had applied for the Criminal Division, which has no connection at all with his IT degree,

candidates cleared the way to the National Court bench thanks to what can only be termed their extraordinary performance during the one-on-one meeting with the members of the CJT and, not coincidentally, all of them have obvious links to *correísmo*.

First of all, Wilson Andino, a brother of Alianza PAIS Assembly Member Mauro Andino, scored 8.5 points in his interview. This enabled him to jump from 33rd to 18th place and into a seat on the National Court. He is currently writing the Court's opinion in the controversial Chevron case.

Janeth Santamaría, who at some point in time had worked with Alianza PAIS Assembly Member Paola Pabón, received a 9.5 score in her final interview and was thus able to move from 55th to 41st place and earn a seat as an associate justice.

The interview round was a scheme used by *correísmo* to pack the National Court with its creatures. No review was possible and the scoring was wholly subjective. It was deftly placed at the very end of the selection process, by which time the members of the Transitional Council of the Judicature already knew how many points each candidate needed to move to the bench,

This final interview or hearing had three elements:

1. The candidate's rationale for wishing to be a justice of the National Court, with a possible maximum score of three points.

2. The candidate's experience, with a possible maximum score of two points; and

3. The candidate's views on the administration of justice, with a possible maximum score of five points.

Career judges like Yolanda Yupanqui or Edgar Flores Mier should, therefore, have received at least one point for each of these three aspects. Inexplicably, they received the lowest scores of all candidates: 1.3 in the case of Yupanqui and 1.2 in the case of Flores Mier (Exhibit 14). Indeed, Flores Mier held 14th place at the end of the first round, prior to the final interview, and was deprived of his seat on the National Court by a score wholly inconsistent with the knowledge and expertise he had demonstrated during that oral hearing.

There are still more cases. An article published in *Hoy* summarizes them.[24] There is the case of Luis Quiroz, a judge also involved in the *El Universo* case. He leapfrogged from dead last (64th place) to 48th thanks to his 9.60 score in the one-on-one meeting. And although that was not good enough to earn him an appointment as an associate justice, Fernando Yávar, a member of the Transitional Council of the Judicature, announced the possibility that the number of associate justices might be increased, leaving Quiroz with a latent expectation that finally came true when he was appointed associate justice to hear some of the Court's overload cases.

Also deprived of the possibility of joining the highest court in the land except, perhaps, as associate judges, were the distinguished jurist from Ambato, Rosa Álvarez, and attorneys Richard Villagómez and Gustavo Durango. Indeed, Durango's score at the final meeting caused him to slip four places.

---

24. *Hoy*, "Una audiencia cambió todo" ["One hearing changed everything"], January 29, 2012.

For his part, José Terán dropped so low, from 18th to 39th place that he was altogether left out of the running for justice and alternate justice positions.

CJT Chairman Paulo Rodríguez's explanation for all these cases was that the grade for the final round was "final." What Rodríguez failed to mention is that the Judicial Branch is governed, as far as procedure is concerned, by Public Administration Organic Law, as contemplated in the third subparagraph of paragraph 4 of Article 3 of said statute and that, therefore, the provisions of Article 65, titled "Assuming a public position," are determining. Paragraph 3 of said article clearly and expressly provides the following: "Grades in competitions on qualifications must be assigned using objective parameters and in no event may the nominating authorities intervene directly or subjectively or make use of discretionary mechanisms. This type of irregularities shall invalidate personnel selection processes."

In other words, the members of the Transitional Council of the Judicature acted against an express provision since, in their capacity as nominating authorities, they intervened directly in the selection process for justices of the National Court of Justice, administering an oral test that was not only wholly subjective but also constituted a discretionary mechanism. Therefore, seen in the light of the aforementioned statute, those proceedings are of no value as they were invalidated by the behavior of the members of the Transitional Council of the Judicature.

3

Baltasar Garzón's International Monitoring Commission

The Correa government thought it advisable to create an International Monitoring Commission to bestow legitimacy on the outcome of the judicial reform process the Transitional Council of the Judicature had been conducting. But as time was of the essence for this new attempt to mess with the judiciary, five months after the referendum that resulted in the creation of the Transitional Council of the Judicature a cooperation agreement was signed in Quito between the Ministry of Justice and the Citizen Participation and Social Monitoring Council for the creation of an International Monitoring Commission.[25]

A little over a month later, on November 27, 2011, the International Monitoring Commission for the Reform of the Judicial Branch was finally installed in Quito. As stat-

25. In another odd coincidence, the agreement was signed on October 20, 2011, the same day the office of the finance manager of the Ministry of Justice, Human Rights, and Worship certified that there were sufficient funds in its coffers to set up such an entity to impart greater legitimacy to the process. The funds would be allocated from the Judicial Branch's overall communications project. The agreement, with a budget of USD 555,770, was signed by Johanna Pesántez and Marcela Miranda on behalf, respectively, of the aforementioned government departments.

ed in the monitors' undertaking, this body was created as an "independent, deliberative, and transparent mechanism to assist Ecuadorian State institutions in evaluating the implementation of said reform."

According to this same document, the major duties of the International Monitoring Commission were two:

1. Acquainting itself with the background, reality, and unfolding of the Judicial Branch and the reform thereof through documents, pertinent data, and direct conversations with organizations, individuals, and institutions such as the government, the National Assembly, the Council of the Judicature, the Office of the Attorney General of the Republic, the Public Defender's Office, judges, bar associations, political parties, different sectors of the economy, and civil society organizations.

2. Preparing two progress reports on the work being done by the International Monitoring Commission, and a final report that would include an assessment of the information gleaned and the monitor reasoned opinions and recommendations, which would be made available to all institutions and the population at large.

This commitment document was signed by all members of the International Monitoring Commission, the final makeup of which was as follows:

Baltasar Garzón Real – A former Spanish magistrate and advisor to The Hague International Criminal Court, born in Jaén, Andalucia, on October 26, 1955. Garzón holds some 20 honorary degrees from universities all over the world. His record includes investigations into terrorist and drug-trafficking organizations, and the issuance of an arrest warrant against former Chilean dictator

Augusto Pinochet for crimes against humanity. He was appointed coordinator of the Ecuadorian International Monitoring Commission for the Reform of the Judicial Branch. Since then he has been defense counsel for Julian Assange, of Wikileaks fame, who on August 16, 2012, sought asylum in the Ecuadorian embassy in London, where he still remains.

Carolina Escobar Sarti – A Guatemalan, born on December 11, 1960, with over 20 years of experience as a teacher and investigator in the field of social studies. As an opinion journalist, she has written for, and appeared at, dozens of media outlets in Guatemala. She is the recipient of several awards, including a UNICEF prize for her work in communications. She was appointed assistant coordinator to the International Monitoring Commission.

Porfirio Muñoz Ledo – A Mexican politician and several-time congressman, born in Mexico City on July 23, 1933. As a member of the Institutional Revolutionary Party (PRI), he held numerous public positions. He left the PRI to help found the Democratic Revolution Party (PRD) and has been closely identified with Andrés Manuel López Obrador, a former presidential candidate and a well-known man of the left. Although Muñoz Ledo accepted the appointment, he explained that because of his many responsibilities, he would permanently delegate his duties on Gustavo Vela, an expert in constitutional issues and a professor at Mexico' National Autonomous University.

Rafael Follonier – An 1970s Argentine left-wing activist, an expert in international affairs and well-known print and television journalist. An article published in *La Nación* (Argentina) on April 18, 2010, described him in these terms:

... he presently holds the rather pompous title of Technical Affairs Coordinator for the Office of the President. But, in practical terms, he has been the Kirchners' trusted man, their shadow foreign minister, a low-profile negotiator who clinches deals with street protestor groups, and a skilful political operator for left-wing *kirchnerismo*, with a unique background as a revolutionary militant in the seventies ...

This monitor did not become actively involved in the Commission's work, however, and delegated his duties on Daniel Gurzi and Víctor Foresi, both of whom enjoy his trust and have had experience in political matters.

Marco Aurelio Garcia – A Brazilian politician and member of the Labor Party headed by former President Lula da Silva. He was acting president of Brazil between October 6, 2006, and January 2, 2007. He is an expert in international affairs.

Merigen Hornkohl – A Chilean politician, born on September 25, 1953. She was secretary of state in President Michelle Bachelet's first administration and Chile's ambassador to Germany.

Another attempt to obfuscate
In an effort to cover up the multifarious irregularities that had plagued the selection process for justices of the new National Court of Justice, the government, an old hand at this game after six years in power, set up a so-called National Monitoring Commission. But in a cynical admission of the true intent of this parallel (and clearly redundant) monitoring process, it was entrusted to Alianza PAIS Al-

ternate Assembly Member Rodrigo Collaguazo. This man has had occasion to take part in National Assembly sessions and is a well-known militant in the government's political arm (Exhibit 24). Baltasar Garzón was given documentation showing the farcical nature of his appointment, and any opinions expressed by Collaguazo were disqualified. The incident highlighted, however, the government's attempt to legitimize the selection process with this shameful maneuver.

Baltasar Garzón is handed the evidence for my complaints

On Thursday, March 15, 2012, at a one-on-one meeting in Quito with Baltasar Garzón, coordinator of the International Monitoring Commission for the Reform of the Judicial Branch lasting approximately 45 minutes, I made available to the Spanish jurist the main facts revealed by my investigation into the selection process for justices of the National Court. The documentary information was handed over in a binder that included all documents in support of my complaint, such as the college degrees of Mariana Yumbay, Wilson Merino, Ximena Vintimilla, and Paúl Íñiguez, and the issues raised by the CJT's personal interviews with Lucy Blacio, Johnny Ayluardo, and Wilson Andino, among other recently anointed justices.

I made a special effort to explain to Garzón how individuals lacking the necessary merits were nevertheless eased into the new high court. I pointed out that, as a result of the contorted methods used to favor these individuals, other, undoubtedly better qualified candidates, had been excluded.

In my conversation with the former Spanish magistrate I explained the obstacles my investigation had run into. In the first place, the candidates' documents had been removed from the CJT's webpage and all attempts to access them electronically had been to no avail, in clear violation of the transparency that ought to have been the hallmark of the entire process.

As he concluded our meeting, Garzón assured me that he would carefully peruse the documentation I had submitted. When the International Monitoring Commission published its three reports, I ascertained that he had indeed reviewed the documentation and verified that my complaints were well grounded.

I subsequently met again with Garzón in Guayaquil and handed him new information on the matter. It should be said that the International Monitoring Commission was always willing to entertain my objections and review their supporting evidence.

Finally, on the eve of the submission of their final report, I met one last time with Garzón and his team of international monitors. The meeting took place at the Marriott Hotel in Quito. The documents they were handed took the monitors by surprise.

4

What the government
could not hide

On August 9, 2011, two months before the International
Monitoring Commission was set up, Justice Minister Johanna Pesántez wrote to Baltasar Garzón inviting him to
join this body that would monitor the reform of the justice
system in Ecuador.

The reform, Pesántez explained in the first two paragraphs of her letter, had been made possible by the May
7, 2011, referendum and popular consultation. She added
that the restructuring process would last 18 months.

In her third paragraph, the minister of justice praised
Garzón's record:

> ...your enormous experience in the field of justice and
> your transcendental contributions to human rights, im-
> provements to justice delivery systems, the recovery of
> historical truth, and the strengthening of democracies,
> have endowed you with a kind of public and ethical
> knowledge that it essential to the sensitive and exten-
> sive process of restructuring the justice system Ecuador
> is driving forward today" [sic].

It is only in the fourth paragraph of her missive that
the distinguished jurist Johanna Pesántez gets around to

disclosing one of the key elements of this process. She tells the former Spanish judge that his presence would be "a significant contribution to our government," and goes on to affirm that "the reports prepared by the top management team will be confidential and for the exclusive use of the Executive" [sic]. If this was to be so, what benefits could the country expect from a monitoring commission whose results would be secret? Fortunately, Pesántez's affirmation did not go beyond a statement of governmental intent, and the International Monitoring Commission eventually published three partial and one final report.

Indeed, the many substantial doubts surrounding this *correísta* judicial reform process were further highlighted and underscored by the International Monitoring Commission's reports. Keeping those reports secret would have been a grievous mistake, as Baltasar Garzón no doubt realized..

The IMC's first preliminary report

The first preliminary report of the International Monitoring Committee led by Baltasar Garzón was made public in the afternoon of Friday, May 11, 2012. The 102-page document was handed to Fernando Cedeño, acting chairman of the Citizen Participation and Social Monitoring Council; Paulo Rodríguez, chairman of the Transitional Council of the Judicature; and Johanna Pesántez, Minister of Justice, Human Rights, and Worship.

At the event, Garzón made emphasis on the IMC's independence, underlining the fact that it had not been subjected to pressures from any government or private organization.

The report begins with an explanation of the background and context of the judicial restructuring process. There is a chronological review of the work done by the monitors, listing all entities or organizations they had spoken with, including, among others, the Truth Commission's Victims Association, the Bar Association of Pichincha, the Public Defender's Office, the Office of the Attorney General of the Republic, the National Assembly's Collective Rights Commission, the National Higher Studies Institute, local monitoring committees, and social and political organizations.

Below is a literal transcription of a summary of the problems affecting some sectors of society — part of an X-ray image of the state of the Judicial Branch — and the solutions proposed by the monitors:

National Court: justices, associate justices, recording secretaries, and chief clerks

Problems:

Pursuant to the provisions of the Organic Code of the Judicial Branch, the makeup of the specialized divisions was not the most suitable, as there are not enough specialized justices.

This lack of specialization means that only justices knowledgeable in each area do the actual work while the others defer to their decisions.

The number of specialized judges and their respective divisions has no practical rationale behind it, as only one single specialized division is created and the assignment of cases to minidivisions only complicates their handling.

The divisions with the heavier workload, i.e., the civil, criminal, and labor divisions, currently lack justices specialized in those fields.

The challenges phase of the selection process for justices and associate judges of the National Court of Justice was not adequate and lacked clear rules.

The final hearing or oral interview with members of the Council of the Judicature was quite subjective.

Proposals

Legal reforms must be made to the Organic Code of the Judicial Branch with respect to the makeup of specialized divisions, assignment of cases, number of divisions, work done by justices and associate justices, the creation of district administrative law and tax courts.

Mandatory conciliation procedures should be created for all matters so as to reduce the number of litigious cases that make their way to the National Court of Justice.

Article 106 of the Organic Code of the Judicial Branch, allowing the sanctioning of judicial servants at any time, should be repealed or amended.

Indigenous movements

Problems:

Criminalization of social protest and persecution of indigenous leaders by the different state attorney's offices of the country, which evidence the involvement of the Executive Branch in these activities.

There are no indigenous judges, i.e., the intercultural and plurinational State required by the constitution is not being developed.

The Public Safety Act allows the Armed Forces to involve themselves in what ought to be off-limits areas of indigenous peoples and nationalities.

Indigenous jurisdiction is not allowed to be respected by the Ecuadorian State.

There is no previous consultation and no pre-legislative consultation. This is one of the most serious problems, one that has helped mobilize the indigenous sector.

Indigenous peoples and nationalities have not been consulted with or involved in the reform of the justice system.

Proposals

There should be greater participation by indigenous peoples and nationalities in the makeup of courts at all levels.

Priority must be given to the Indigenous and Regular Justice Coordination and Cooperation Act, but no actions denoting superiority should be permitted, such as the execution of cooperation agreements, as those actions ought to arise out of the respect existing between both justice systems.

Indigenous leaders should cease to be persecuted for crimes of sabotage and terrorism,

A previous and pre-legislative consultation law must be passed, and the decisions of indigenous peoples and nationalities with respect to mining processes and laws affecting them must be respected.

Transitional Council of the Judicature

Coordination meeting – Commitments

The appointment of associate justices at the request of sitting justices should not be allowed; in the past, this was a highly controversial and discretionary practice, at loggerheads with a selection process based on qualifications and competition.

In coordination with the National Assembly, legal reforms will be proposed to the Organic Code of the Judicial Branch with a view to preventing cases from becoming backlogged.

A commitment is made to revise Article 106 of the Organic Code of the Judicial Branch which allows the sanctioning of judicial servants at any time.

With respect to the previous point, the Monitoring Commission proposes: that the power to sanction judicial servants at any time the appropriate authorities learn [of the circumstances motivating the sanction] be repealed; rather, that such sanctioning be limited exclusively to the moment when the administrative malfeasance occurred. At the same time, an administrative sanction should be established and disciplinary records purged so as not to impede the servant's judicial career in the future.

Judicial Branch

Problems

No culture of evaluation processes existed, nor were [judges] allowed to contribute with the fruits of their accumulated experience in the institution.

As regards talent, the experience of judicial servants has not been taken into account.

They do not oppose evaluation but object to the fact that evaluations were not done in accordance with the performance of their permanent activities. There was no previous professional profile.

Vacancies are not filled through selection processes based on competition and qualifications but, rather, through temporary contracts.

What took place was not a judicial evaluation but, instead, a large-scale restructuring.

Judges and all other servants have not been trained at a judicial school.

Judicial training was imparted only to certain individuals, with the result that not all personnel members were prepared for these evaluations.

There is no incentive system; only a mechanism for grievances and sanctions.

The Transitional Council of the Judicature is in the hands of the Executive Branch.

Once the evaluations of judicial servants have been weighed, there is no confidence in the reconsiderations that have taken place.

Removals from the bench must also be taken into account. Therefore, if the evaluations are added, the number of judicial servants who have been removed is quite high, not taking into account those who have been dropped from the lists.

There is no severance pay in cases of removal from the bench.

Judges have been removed from the bench for having issued jurisdictional resolutions. This situation cannot be allowed, as there are horizontal and vertical legal remedies, in addition to the fact that this alleged malfeasance is prohibited under the Organic Code of the Judicial Branch.

Proposals

To create a culture of periodic evaluation processes in the judiciary.

The Ecuadorian State ought to address the concerns raised by the United Nations Office of the Special Rapporteur on the Independence of Judges and Lawyers.

Judicial independence and impartiality should be fostered.

Periodic meetings should be held with the international bar associations system at any of its levels or mandates.

Critical obstacles encountered by the IMC

The international team monitoring the judicial reform process encountered two critical obstacles in the process, to wit:

1. Selection, designation, and makeup of the National Court of Justice of Ecuador;
2. Evaluation of judicial servants in Ecuador.

Selection, designation, and makeup of the National Court of Justice

The first doubt raised by the International Monitoring Commission had to do with the impossibility of following up on the selection process in real time. All three members of the CJT delayed producing the necessary information. This problem is addressed in the IMC document.

But the International Monitoring Commission headed by Baltasar Garzón also harbored serious doubts as to the makeup of the highest court in the land. This chapter of its report explains that complaints were received from Assembly Members Andrés Páez and Paco Moncayo and that both were invited to share their concerns and asked to submit information supporting their allegations.

The monitors added that their own investigative team conducted inquiries which provided the basis for a confidential report. The IMC corroborated all the complaints I voiced, as summarized below:

With respect to my complaint regarding Justice Mariana Yumbay Yallico, the monitors found that, in fact, she had received her law degree from the Central University of Ecuador on March 15, 2011, and that, consequently, she had been practicing law for exactly ten years and six months at the time her candidacy was submitted. This, the monitors noted, did not entitle her to the six points she was awarded in her final score.

The IMC went on to say that the award of two points could be understood if the Transitional Council of the Judicature had taken the six months as the equivalent of one year, but that in no event could the awarding of six points be justified (Exhibit 20).

It is interesting to note that the IMC elicited Yumbay's opinion on this issue. According to the report, she said she had asked CJT member Tania Arias that same day about the grading method in the qualifications stage and that Arias had told her that it was an "interpretation" of her professional experience, ordered and decided by the Expert Committee, and that the same criterion had been applied to 200 other candidates.

IMC Chairman Baltasar Garzón raised this concern with Arias, who explained she had referred to a verbal report from the aforesaid Expert Committee authorizing the awarding of additional points to Yumbay. Garzón then requested a written report on Arias's statement. The report was submitted and it coincides exactly with what the CJT member had said. The monitors deemed it necessary to hear the Expert Committee's opinion[26] and the issue was left pending.[27]

The cases of Lucy Blacio and Yolanda Yupanqui were reviewed next, also on the basis of the complaints I submitted on March 15, 2012. Here, the irregular behavior occurred during their personal interviews with the members of the Transitional Council of the Judicature, where Blacio received a perfect score (10/10) while Yupanqui, with no justification, was assigned an exceedingly low grade (1.3/10).

Following the monitors' review of this case, they concluded that it was never possible to establish what the basis was for the CJT to assign those scores to the two candidates.

The preliminary report next takes up the case of Wilson Merino, a justice who, as I stated in my complaint, had inexplicably been awarded ten points in the qualifications stage while irregularities in his professional credentials had been overlooked.

The monitors found that Merino never established his professional experience, as he failed to submit copies of pleadings or judgments showing his involvement as attorney of record. All he produced was a certificate from the Bar Association of Azuay and a taxpayer's registration form showing his employment as an instructor but not as a free-lance practicing lawyer.

---

26. This is reflected in the International Monitoring Committee's first report and is reiterated in its final report.

27. I will later address the Expert Committee's performance.

The report also states that, asked to explain why he wished to be a National Court justice, Merino rambled on about human rights, the Pachamama, water rights, and other extraneous issues, a performance that certainly called into question the inordinately high score he was awarded for his one-on-one meeting with the CJT.

In the case involving Wilson Andino, a brother of Alianza PAIS Assembly Member Mauro Andino, the international monitors found that, had it not been for the 8.5/10 score he was awarded for his personal interview, he would not have been able to leapfrog from 33rd to 18th place, edging out Edgar Flores, a jurist who, as already mentioned, only received a paltry 1.2 grade from the Transitional Council of the Judicature.

The report objected to two features of the oral hearing: that it took place at the end of the selection process, when scores in the previous stages were already a matter of public knowledge, and that it was given a weight of ten points, a disproportionate figure when the subjective nature of the test is considered.

The first preliminary report ended with a listing of criteria for evaluating judges, underscoring the need to respect the basic rights of judicial servants.

The IMC's second preliminary report

The International Monitoring Commission submitted its second preliminary report on August 9, 2012. The document reviewed compliance with the first report's recommendations and reported on the inspection to ascertain the progress achieved in the construction of new buildings for the Judicial Branch throughout the country and the re-modeling of existing structures.

As this 72-page document reflects, the Transitional Council of the Judicature had reported progress, especially with respect to the establishment of parameters for the handling of judicial servants' grievances and incentives as well as clearly defined disciplinary mechanisms.

But, as regards the independence of the judiciary, the report notes no government commitment, and the monitors themselves ask instead that judicial independence be respected.

The following is a literal transcription of what Baltasar Garzón's commission wrote on the subject:

> The International Monitoring Commission is of the opinion that although the aim is not to generate dependence by the Judicial Branch on other State branches, it is nevertheless important to exhort or urge all other State branches to respect judicial independence — without prejudice in any event of the right to criticize court decisions — on the basis of the review of jurisdictional decisions through existing ordinary and extraordinary remedies.
>
> The International Monitoring Commission is aware that the defense of judicial independence is not incumbent upon any management model but, rather, an obligation of each and every one of the citizens and institutions of the State. For this reason, the Transitional Council of the Judicature must be the guarantor of judicial independence against any kind of external or internal meddling, attempted through the hypothetical use of administra-

tive sanctions that could directly or indirectly interfere with the judges' exercise of the jurisdictional function.

In page five of the second preliminary report, the International Monitoring Commission notes — and it is important to highlight this — that in both the selection process for justices of the National Court and competitions 101 and 313 for lower court judges "diverse instructions have been implemented that modified the original rules and regulations." Here is further evidence that irregularities were also committed in this way and that the government succeeded in manipulating the process for designating judges at all levels.

The lies Garzón was told

A liar is sooner caught than a cripple, the saying goes. The International Monitoring Commission was unabashedly lied to about compliance with the recommendations made in its first preliminary report. The CJT led Baltasar Garzón's team to believe that many of its suggestions had already been taken into account and even implemented. But the documentation I gathered during my investigation of the judicial reform process exposed some of the lies told by the government. Two clear examples of this governmental mendacity are discussed next.[28]

---

28. Answers to my requests in connection with this issue were provided under cover of Official Communication No. 2301-DG-CJ-12-SEP issued by the CJT on September 14, 2012. Tania Arias's report is included in the IMC's first preliminary report as well as in its final report.

In their first preliminary report, the international monitors recommended filling court vacancies at a set time so as to afford greater security to judicial servants. The Transitional Council of the Judicature answered that an administrative resolution to that effect had been issued on May 31, 2012, thus complying with the IMC's recommendation. But since the resolution in question was not appended to the CJT's response, the monitors opted to remain silent on the subject. For my part, I demanded to be given a copy of this administrative resolution, allegedly issued on the aforementioned date. The answer I received was that "there was no meeting of the full Council of the Judicature on May 31, 2012" (Exhibit 20).

On page 64 of its second preliminary report, the International Monitoring Commission notes with displeasure that the CJT had not addressed "the possibility of accessing personal documents such as examinations and tests, even though in the report contained in memorandum No. 28-CJ-JIA-2012, Inter-institutional Coordinator Paulina Palacios admits that they must be produced for the sake of transparency." I subpoenaed a copy of said memorandum signed by Paulina Palacios but the Transitional Council of the Judicature replied that "… we clarify that this subpoena is in error, as there is no memorandum meeting that description in the archives of the office of Inter-institutional Coordination" (Exhibit 20).

In that same report, the International Monitoring Commission several times expresses its unhappiness with the CJT's non-responsive answers to questions and objections. In other words, the members of the Transitional Council of the Judicature had no qualms in lying to the

International Monitoring Committee to please their boss in Carondelet Palace.

The report makes special emphasis on the selection process for 1,284 judges and 532 notaries. The International Monitoring Commission notes that, even though the process had been closed,[29] the CJT nevertheless took the unusual step of reopening it with the excuse of an alleged "errata sheet." This expedient was questioned by the IMC, as the Transitional Council of the Judicature had frequently used this artifice to favor certain candidates. The international monitors also pointed out that extemporaneous notices were used to prevent certain candidates from uploading their sworn statements to the CJT's webpage as the system had shut down.

Even more significant are the IMC's objections to the grading parameters. While qualifications were assigned 15 points, and 65 points were given for the candidates' performance in the competitive examinations, 20 points were set aside for their initial professional training. This prompted the international monitors to observe that "these parameters are disproportionate as regards the weight given qualifications, which are the result of each candidate's training and experience, gained through the time, effort, and dedication of the individual candidates. The theoretical test and the candidate's educational, which have a combined weight of 60 points [sic], could lend themselves to a discretionary or subjective evaluation of his or her qualifications. Consequently, transparency mechanisms must be identified and adopted to guarantee equal oppor-

---

29. It so stated on page 60 of the third preliminary report..

tunity to all candidates in accordance with constitutional principles."[30]

The International Monitoring Commission was clearly hinting that these selection processes for judges and justices lacked transparency and that, once again, the Transitional Council of the Judicature was availing itself of subjective and discretionary mechanisms to favor certain candidates identified with the *correísta* regime to the detriment of better qualified candidates. This shows that the government not only "messed with" the lofty circles of the National Court of Justice but also with the lower courts, making sure that nothing evaded control by Carondelet Palace.

The IMC's third preliminary report

This last preliminary report was submitted on Thursday, November 15. It is a 68-page document, signed by Baltasar Garzón as coordinator general of the International Monitoring Commission; Marigen Hohnkohl, international monitor; and Víctor Hugo Foresi on behalf of International Monitor Rafael Follonier.

After summing up the IMC's work since the second preliminary report, the international monitors describe the meetings they held with different actors in the judiciary.

Special attention is paid to their meeting with the families of "The Luluncoto Ten," ten young people jailed and charged with terrorism. The government's only evidence against them was the possession of CDs and books by Che Guevara.

According to the report, the international monitors were able to meet several times with relatives of the de-

---

30.; Page 62 of the IMC's third preliminary report

tained young people and spoke once to one of them. But the IMC stated that it "is not a judicial or extrajudicial investigative body, and cannot interfere with the activities incumbent upon the Judicial Branch" [sic].

At the end, however, the report makes reference to the concern this controversial case raises with the IMC and points out that "after learning of the charges, and respecting judicial independence as a determining element of the Judicial Branch itself, we express our concern over facts the legal and criminal description of which is based on an old law and on a factual basis that does not comport in the least with the severity of the punishment contemplated for that behavior" [sic].

The International Monitoring Commission then formulates 38 recommendations that the Ecuadorian State is at liberty to adopt or ignore, as this is a non-binding report. The recommendations dealt with control mechanisms for the National Police (such as the creation of an internal independent body to prevent irregularities), the social rehabilitation system (such as segregating convicts between the ages of 18 and 22 from the rest of the penal population), and the training of judicial servants in the area of human rights..

5

The Expert Committee's role in the selection process for justices of the new National Court

An Expert Committee was created under Article 7 of the Rules and Regulations for the Competition on Qualifications, Citizen Challenges, and Social Monitoring for the Selection and Designation of Judicial Branch Female and Male Servants,[31] and as provided by Articles 4 and 5 of the Instructions for this competition.[32]. Its powers included "reviewing and qualifying the documents submitted by candidates to establish their practice of law with recognized probity or their participation in the judicature or in the university-level teaching of legal sciences for a minimum period of ten (10) years."

The Expert Committee was made up of Remigio Auquilla Lucero, of Azuay University; Carlos García Torres, of the Loja Private Technical University; Sandra Morejón Llanos, of the Espíritu Santo Specialties University; Diego Zalamea León, on behalf of the Council of the Judicature; and María Pavlova Guerra, from the Central University of Ecuador.

---

31. Resolution 006-2011

32. Resolution 007-2011

Diego Zalamea had worked at the National Assembly as advisor to Assembly Member Mauro Andino, a brother of then candidate Wilson Andino, and was actively involved in the deliberations of the Assembly's Justice Commission to which I also belonged. His designation as a member of the Expert Committee violated the provisions of Article 4 of the Instructions which require that the experts be independent, a qualification Zalamea clearly failed to meet.

And while on the subject of the grading of candidates, it is worth noting that this Expert Committee was not empowered to interpret any rules, for that power was vested in the full Transitional Council of the Judicature, as provided in paragraph c of Article 4 of the aforementioned Rules and Regulations. In cases not contemplated in the regulations, the chairman of the Transitional Council of the Judicature was duty bound to consult the full Council, as provided by paragraph c of Article 5 of the Rules and Regulations.

This notwithstanding, the Expert Committee issued an official communication on October 21, 2011 (Exhibit 21), informing the national personnel director of the Transitional Council of the Judicature that "it had been decided to evaluate simultaneously and in cumulative fashion the practice of law and the experience as a member of the judicature or the university-level teaching of the legal sciences inasmuch as the experiences certified by the candidates are complementary (related but not equal) and because this helps determine the length of time candidates have effectively devoted to the law, and allows an inference to be made as to their skills to be justices of the National Court of Justice."

With this pronouncement, the Expert Committee openly contradicted the provisions of paragraph 3 of Article 12 of the Instructions, where the disjunctive "or" is clearly used instead of the conjunctive "and." Consequently, the appropriate course of action was to assign a score on the basis of one parameter and not of all three simultaneously. Withal, it is clear that the requirement to be a candidate was to have at least ten years of professional practice and that any additional points for overall work experience, according to Article 32 of the Instructions, would be awarded for each additional *full* year[33] reckoned as of the tenth year of professional practice, up to a maximum of ten points.

In Official Communication No. 2768-APB-ID-12-DR, dated July 4, 2012, I asked the CJT for an explanation of this decision by the Expert Committee and requested a list showing for each candidate how many points he or she was awarded for university teaching, how many for his or her professional practice, and how many for his or her judicial tenure.

My request was answered through Official Communication No. 1842 of July 20, 2012 (Exhibit 22), which is a key piece of evidence of the irregularities engaged in to favor failing *correísta* candidates.

Indeed, in the case of Mariana Yumbay, she was allowed THIRTEEN YEARS of professional experience, a clear impossibility when one recalls that, being barely ten years out of law school, she could not have practiced law and sat on the bench simultaneously. Without any basis whatsoever and in highly suspicious fashion, the CJT claimed that Yumbay had a simultaneous experience

---

33. This is clearly stipulated in Article 32 of the Instructions.

equivalent to two years, six months, and 15 days, while noting that she had not produced records for any academic experience. In any event, and assuming *arguendo* that the CJT's claims are valid, Yumbay would only have had two full years. Yet, the Transitional Council of the Judicature highhandedly decided to take a fraction of a year into consideration to award her six points.

Something similar occurred in the case of Wilson Merino. Although he had received his law degree barely ten years earlier, the CJT assigned him 15 years, one month, and seven days of experience, with a cumulative experience of four years, eight months, and one day. Once again, Council members considered a fraction of a year as a whole year in order to award him ten points.

It is strikingly odd that what the CJT termed "simultaneous experience" is the exact equivalent of the time it claims the candidate had shown he had devoted to the teaching of law. It is not clear why the CJT failed to take into account Merino's years as a lawyer and a judge, as it did in the Yumbay case. Or to say it differently: CJT members considered Merino's academic experience to award him ten points while, at the same time, ignoring other parameters they had considered in Yumbay's case.

Similar inconsistencies plague the case of Ximena Vintimilla. The CJT arrived at the curious conclusion that she had a simultaneous experience of four years, ten months, and 20 days. Yet, in her case the CJT ignored the fraction of a year and assigned her eight points when in fact she was entitled to only four points, as she had only two full years of legal experience beyond the required ten-year minimum.

So far, no one knows how the Transitional Council of the Judicature calculated the years of "simultaneous experience" or "cumulative experience." But its explanations reveal the manipulation of figures and the deliberate fraud perpetrated to benefit candidates identified with *correísmo*.

It is worth mentioning that both the International Monitoring Commission's first preliminary report and section VI.3.3 of its final report, "Meetings with members of the Expert Committee," reproduce key testimony by Remigio Auquilla, a member of the Expert Committee. Auquilla questioned the final one-on-one meetings and the excessive weight it was given, and pointed out that the members of said Committee "were responsible for 68 of the 100-point score." This disclosed the reality that 32 points were awarded directly by the Transitional Council of the Judicature. Of this 32-point total, ten points were assigned on the basis of the final personal interview, while the remaining 22 are unaccounted for.

But that is not the end of it. Auquilla disclosed that the candidates' personal binders were not reviewed by the Expert Committee but, instead, by subalterns of the CJT triunvirate, all of whom were employees of the Office of the Personnel Director of the Transitional Council of the Judicature.[34]

Auquilla's revelation is quite disturbing:

> … in other words, the Expert Committee did not phys-
> ically review the binders or the documents .." As the
> International Monitoring Commission's final report

---

34. Final Report of the International Monitoring Commission on Judicial Reform in Ecuador, p. 52

states, Auquilla has also stated that the Expert Committee members were called in expressly to grade specific personal experience, which accounted for 10 points, as the remaining 20 points had already been awarded, although not by them."[35]

According to the IMC's final report, Attorney Sandra Morejón, an Expert Committee member, stated that work experience had initially been graded by Human Resources and that Expert Committee members were subsequently handed a certificate to grade specific experience and publications. The IMC corroborated Morejón's statements by noting in its report that she "insisted she had not graded overall work experience."[36]

These revelations prove the Expert Committee was prevented from grading overall work experience, and that this task was performed directly by the Transitional Council of the Judicature, made up of three *correístas*, for the purpose of "messing with" the candidates' qualifications.

Summing up, then: the Expert Committee was responsible for awarding 68 points out of a total of 100. The remaining 32 were left up to a threesome of officials identified with Rafael Correa, and were more than enough to "mess with" the selection process and pave the way to the National Court of Justice for justices prefabricated at Carondelet Palace. This is all the more glaring when one recalls that seats on the highest court in the land were

---

35. Final Report of the International Monitoring Commission on Judicial Reform in Ecuador, p. 53

36. Final Report of the International Monitoring Commission on Judicial Reform in Ecuador, p. 56

ultimately decided by tenths and even hundredths of a point.

I have subpoenaed the testimony of the members of the Expert Committee for the sole purpose of eliciting further evidence to corroborate my complaints. The proceedings, however, are being delayed by procedural tricks played by the proud new masters of the Judicial Branch

6

The International Monitoring
Commission's final report

The International Monitoring Commission's final report
was a bombshell that unleashed an avalanche of criticisms
of the judicial restructuring process. The document hit
the nail on the head. Its 102 pages (not counting Exhibits)
not only validated my complaints but raised objections to
several other procedures used by Correa's much-vaunted
"justice revolution." The report was submitted on November 13, 2012,[37] and triggered controversies at all levels except the highest, as the authorities chose to look elsewhere
and act as if it had nothing to do with them.

At the outset (page 14), the monitors emphasize the
"need to have an autonomous and independent public
entity that guarantees the impartiality of disciplinary controls on judicial servants and removes the menace of in-
tervention on jurisdictional grounds, thereby grievously

---

37. The report was presented barely three hours after the Citizen
Participation and Social Monitoring Council denied with prejudice my challenge of Paulo Rodríguez and Tania Arias, both of
whom were seeking seats in the new Council of the Judicature.
It should be highlighted that the IMC's final report corroborates
the same complaints that provided the basis for my challenge of
these two individuals.

and irreparably attacking judicial independence. No judge may be sanctioned or suspended for interpreting the law." This is a very important part of the report, as it reflects the monitors' concern over the punitive character of the CJT, a body which, according to its own records, handled during its first year of existence more than 900 disciplinary cases, 80% of which resulted in some sort of sanction. How many of those sanctions were the result of court decisions contrary to the government's position, as in the case of Colonel César Carrión?[38]

> This concern is reiterated in page 43 of the report. The monitors criticize the practice of invoking "inexcusable error" in order to levy disciplinary sanctions. Their criticism was couched in the following terms: "... attention should be called to the regulation of the so-called 'inexcusable error' contemplated in the Organic Code of the Judicial Branch. Following investigations conducted by this International Monitoring Commission, it has been established that 'inexcusable error' may be used to disguise disciplinary measures that entail actual judicial reviews. This potential meddling should be eliminated and replaced by a detailed disciplinary system, with defined clauses and the express prohibition of analogous application to the detriment of the alleged responsible official.

The report states that preventive sanctions against judges have become "strictly discretionary measures," masquerading as alleged instances of prevarication.

---

38. Magazine Vanguardia, issue 372, "El modelo judicial de la mano dura" ["The strong-hand judicial model"]

As regards the construction of new buildings, claimed as an iconic achievement by the "citizen revolution", the report records the IMC's uneasiness over "the failure to verify contracting processes [...] and the details of the actual awarding of contracts. This was due to the failure of the Citizen Participation and Social Monitoring Council to designate the necessary officials, despite requests to that effect ..." This issue becomes particularly significant in light of several reports of alleged overpricing in direct contracts. Government regulators have provided no responses to these complaints, despite the documentation submitted in due course by the parties reporting these irregularities.

The IMC's final report also analyses the case of "The Luluncoto Ten," the ten young people arrested on sabotage and terrorism charges. It states that following meetings with social organizations, it was able to ascertain that an extremely harsh criminal statute might have been applied to punish simple citizen protests. The report warns the Ecuadorian State of "the risk involved in stretching criminal law to include other areas beyond what is internationally identified as terrorism."

The National Court of Justice: doubts and objections

The International Monitoring Commission's final report set forth its concerns over the process followed for the designation of National Court justices. The IMC's doubts are based on the complaints I publicly raised, full documentation on which I made available to Baltasar Garzón.

The monitoring entity reviewed the cases of Mariana Yumbay, Lucy Blacio Pereira, Yolanda Yupanqui, Paúl Íñiguez, Wilson Merino, and Wilson Andino. In the case of Yumbay, the international monitors found that she barely met the requirements to present her candidacy, as she had been practicing law for only ten years and six months. This fact alone knocks out the six extra points she was awarded as if she had had a further three years of experience. On the basis of those unjustified six points Attorney Yumbay received a 27/30 score in the qualifications stage. The IMC points out that if her six months beyond the required 10-year minimum had been considered as one full year, she might conceivably have been entitled to two points, but never to the six she was awarded.

As regards the case involving Lucy Blacio and Yolanda Yupanqui, the IMC's report echoes my complaint. The Commission agrees that it was only thanks to her one-on-one meeting that Blacio was able to secure a seat on the highest court in the land. The report notes that Justice Blacio (as she now is) scored 10/10 in the interview while Yupanqui received a paltry 1.33/10 even though at the end of the first stage the former was in 45th place while the latter held 12th place.

Wilson Merino, as will be recalled, was the judge who upheld the $40-million judgment against *El Universo* and is now handling the embezzlement case against former President Abdalá Bucaram, a matter of the utmost interest to the government.

The International Monitoring Commission reiterated its previous finding that Merino was awarded 10 points for professional experience with no justification at all, as he barely met the selection process' minimum requirement for his candidacy to the National Court of Justice to be considered. The monitors could find no reason for the additional points Merino was awarded.

Merino also benefitted from his one-on-one meeting with the members of the Transitional Council of the Judicature. While the candidate had been in 33rd place before his interview, his 8.5/10 score allowed him to climb to 18th. But as Merino moved up, Edgar Flores, who prior to the hearing was in 14th place, sank below the cutoff point for new justices, receiving an inexplicably low 1.2/10 score.

Seeking explanations for these highly suspicious grades, the international monitors met with the Expert Committee involved in the selection process.

The Expert Committee was represented by Remigio Auquilla, a graduate of Azuay University, as previously mentioned. Auquilla claimed that he had always opposed this last phase of the selection process, as it left absolute responsibility for the last — and, as we have seen, decisive— ten points in the hands of the Transitional Council of the Judicature.

In connection with the grading of the candidates' qualifications (Exhibit 23), where points were awarded for non-existing experience in a wholly inexplicable manner, the explanation given the monitors was that they had been flexible when grading because if more severe criteria had been applied, "a lot of people would have been left out of the process."

It should be noted that, in spite of all these anomalies, regulatory entities have not looked into the matter or questioned the process.

Addressing the irregularities and pressures brought to light in the selection process for National Court justices, *Vistazo* magazine published[39] this note:

> On the last Friday in March, the International Monitoring Commission that had monitored the reform of the justice system received highly revealing testimony. A candidate who, although receiving one of the highest scores, was left out of the National Court of Justice, declared that two public officials had offered to enhance his score if he would only return the favor, 'should the government need it.' The candidate received the officials' unexpected visit the same day of his theoretical test. Both introduced themselves as workers at the Council of the Judicature. The IMC established the identity of one of them: he is a lawyer and a public official. 'They told the candidate he was among the better positioned hopefuls, but that he may be lacking a point or two, and that they were in a position to help him during the reconsideration phase,' the testimony states. When the candidate inquired what the price would be for the proffered support, the answer was: 'For the time being, nothing. But should the government need anything, perhaps you could be of assistance.' The candidate rejected the offer. His statement was recorded in the minutes of his meeting with the members of the International Mon-

---

39. Vistazo magazine, issue No. 1089

itoring Commission. This certificate, together with the IMC's final report, is fated to enjoy eternal rest.

The official response

Faced with the questions clearly raised by Baltasar Garzón and his team, President Correa had recourse to his default strategy: victimization. He publicly stated that the media had taken the information out of context to attack him. The president consistently held the position that the monitors' report was a highly positive one for his administration.

"According to the corrupt press, the report questions the process, but that is false [...] They manipulate us and take comments out of context in an attempt to harm the government," Rafael Correa said on Thursday, December 27, at the opening of the Community Police Unit in Laso, Province of Cotopaxi.

His reaction was to be expected. Garzón's report came at a most inopportune time. Carondelet Palace spinmeisters had not reckoned with the final report being submitted precisely on the eve of a new electoral campaign.

In any event, there is nothing new in Correa ignoring or choosing to sidestep the criticisms of all monitoring committees, including, paradoxically, even those set up by himself.

Early in his administration, in an ostensibly laudable move, he ordered the creation of a monitoring commission charged with determining who were the people responsible for the 1999 banking crisis. The task was entrusted to Eduardo Valencia, a prestigious economist, a professor at the Pontifical Catholic University of Ecuador (PUCE), and an ideologue of the "citizen revolution". But after an investigation lasting a few months, the results were stealthily turned over to the state attorney's office, which failed to act on them. Valencia, in obvious disagreement with the president, had to leave the government and Correa never wished to publicly discuss the issue.

A monitoring commission was next set up to look into the Angostura bombing on March 1, 2008. The person chosen for that task was Francisco Huerta Montalvo, a respected Ecuadorian politician, a man of with an unsullied reputation for honesty. Following an investigation, Huerta reported that the camp where F.A.R.C. guerrilla leader "Raúl Reyes" had been killed also housed a facility for the forging of identity cards for guerrillas. The government never took any action and Huerta had to leave the monitoring commission. Today he is one of the government's most vehement critics.

And then there was a monitoring commission charged with looking into the contracts executed by Fabricio Correa, the president's brother. Pablo Chambers was appointed to lead the commission. After an investigation lasting several months, Chambers confirmed that Rafael Correa indeed had knowledge of his brother's contracts with the government. This report resulted in Chambers and all other members of the monitoring commission having to seek political asylum in different countries following the president's threats to haul them into criminal court.

So, with a president in the habit of setting up monitoring commissions only to ignore or pay no heed to their results, the Citizen Participation and Social Monitoring Council took upon itself the responsibility of answering the wave of criticisms in the wake of Baltasar Garzón's report. Its response was a Kafkaesque one: the creation of a monitoring commission to monitor the International Monitoring Commission.

Sure enough, the monitoring and transparency body proceeded to announce the creation of a monitoring commission to monitor the suggestions made by the International Monitoring Commission. In other words, the government again applied its tried and true technique of legitimating any decision through entities created by the government itself which, should they fail to act to the government's liking, are impugned or simply ignored.

The Citizen Participation Council response could not have been different. This body, it will be recalled, is chaired by Fernando Cedeño, Alianza PAIS's treasurer during the 2006 campaign. Its former chairperson, Marcela Miranda, is an intimate friend of Ricardo Patiño, who even promoted her to the position of chairperson of De todas [All Women's], one of his cooperatives. Then there is Tatiana Ordeñana, once Patiño's subaltern when he headed the Shoreline Ministry. Mónica Banegas, a former consultant to the Ministry of Justice, rounds out the government's majority in the Citizen Participation Council. Luis Pachala, David Rosero, and Andrea Rivera are not aligned with Alianza PAIS and represent the minority in the Citizen Participation Council; their opinions have seldom been taken into account.

But when it comes to arrant nonsense, nothing beats Engineer Paulo Rodríguez. Applauding the decision to set up a monitoring commission to monitor the International Monitoring Commission, Rodriguez insisted that the designation of National Court justices had been "transparent." Tania Arias put the icing on the cake when she stated: "As far as the Council of the Judicature is concerned, the National Court of Justice is legitimate, elected within the constitutional framework. For the Council of the Judicature, this case is closed."[40] Or, to say it in plain language: regardless of what the International Monitoring Commission set up by the government itself may say, Correa had swept its report under the carpet, as if doubts and irregularities could be buried by the opinion of two scandalously incompetent officials who know full well what they must conceal lest they are expelled from the *correísta* Garden of Eden for not being faithful to the official gospel of obsequiousness and unquestionable loyalty to the "Project."

---

40. Vistazo magazine, issue No. 1089

7

Articles of Impeachment against the Transitional Council of the Judicature

With the support of 37 cosponsors in the National Assembly, I proceeded to file articles of impeachment against the three members of the Transitional Council of the Judicature. In so doing, I was exercising my rights and obligations as a citizen and an Assembly member, enshrined in the following constitutional and statutory provisions:

Constitution

Article 83, paragraphs 1 and 7. Without prejudice of others contemplated in the Constitution and the laws, the following are duties and responsibilities of Ecuadorians of both sexes:

1) To abide by and comply with the Constitution, the laws, and the legitimate decisions of competent authorities.

2) To promote the commonweal and give preference to the general interest over the private one in accordance with good living.

Article 120, paragraph 9. In addition to those others determined by law, the National Assembly shall have the following attributions and powers:

9) To monitor the actions of the Executive, Electoral, and Transparency and Social Monitoring Branches, and of the other organs of public power, and to request from public servants such information as it may deem necessary.

Article 131. Its pertinent part provides: *The National Assembly, at the request of at least one fourth of its members, may proceed to impeach State ministers [...] the Council of the Judicature ... for failure to discharge the functions assigned to them under the Constitution and the laws during their term of office and for up to one year after the conclusion thereof.*

Article 181, paragraphs 3 and 5. *In addition to those others determined by law, the following shall be functions of the Council of the Judicature:*

3) To direct the processes for the selection of judges and other servants of the Judicial Branch, and to evaluate, promote, and sanction them. All processes shall be public and decisions shall set forth their grounds.

5) To ensure transparency and efficiency in the Judicial Branch.

Article 179. *When joining the Judicial Branch, the criteria of equality, fairness, probity, competition, qualifications, publicity, challenges, and citizen participation shall be observed.*

Organic Law of the Legislative Branch

Article 74. *Political monitoring and controls are incumbent upon Assembly members, specialized commissions, and the National Assembly as a whole, in accordance with the provisions in the Constitution of the republic, the present law, and the appropriate internal rules and regulations.*

Article 78. *The National Assembly may proceed to impeach the officials listed on Article 131 of the Constitution* *of the republic for failure to discharge the functions assigned to them under the Constitution of the republic and the laws during their term of office and for up to one year after the conclusion thereof.*

Article 254. *The Council of the Judicature is the sole governing, administrative, monitoring, and sanctioning organ of the Judicial Branch, which includes: jurisdictional organs, administrative organs, ancillary organs, and autonomous organs. The Council of the Judicature is an instrumental organ to ensure the correct, efficient, and coordinated operation of jurisdictional, autonomous, and ancillary organs. In no event shall the Council of the Judicature be deemed hierarchically superior to, nor may it attempt against the independence to exercise the specific functions of, judges, prosecutors, and public defenders.*

Article 255, paragraphs 1 and 3. *In addition to those others determined by the Constitution and the laws, members of the Council of the Judicature may be impeached on the following grounds:*

3) Manifest invalidity in the performance of their functions.

Rules and regulations for the competition on qualifications, citizen challenges, and social monitoring for the selection of female and male servants of the Judicial Branch

The principles of equality, probity, non discrimination, publicity, competition, and qualifications, as well as those of citizen participation, social monitoring, transparency, and access to public information shall be observed in the competitions on qualifications to join the Judicial Branch, except as regards the psychological evaluation, which shall be confiden-

tial for the sake of privacy. In matters not expressly contem-
plated here, and in the event of any doubts as to the applica-
tion or construction of the norms established in the present
Rules and Regulations, decisions shall favor the validity of
the competition and the participation of the candidates.

The articles of impeachment were introduced on June 1, 2010. They were based on the irregularities in the selection process for justices of the National Court of Justice fully evidenced by my investigations. The articles of impeachment against the Transitional Council of the Judicature's notorious threesome consist of 50 pages and more than 120 exhibits, and were submitted in printed and digital versions.

But a few weeks later, the Legislative Administrative Council (CAL) dismissed without explanation these articles of impeachment and failed to provide a rationale for the refusal to act on them. The CAL is dominated by *correístas*, who cast four of its seven votes. Its chairman is Fernando Cordero, who is also the speaker of the Legislative Branch, and a member of Alianza PAIS. As was to be expected, the order issued by the government was to ignore any and all complaints and protect the perpetrators of the serious irregularities brought to light, which the International Monitoring Commission's report would shortly confirm.

PART II

HISTORICAL BACKGROUND

8

Modern democracies
and the separation of powers

Democracy is the political and social system closest to perfect coexistence in any country. Democracy is also a concept in whose name societies have been torn asunder in constant clashes and struggles. Democracy evokes strong feelings of human coexistence, especially in places where material and spiritual differences have resulted in unequal societies whose members must either coexist in harmony or destroy themselves.

In its most immediate meaning, democracy represents the possibility that the governed and those who govern them may come to understand one another and peacefully share the same geographic and historic space. But for this to be possible, it is necessary to establish social mechanisms that will enable democratic coexistence.

Democracy is indeed a way of organizing groups in society, and its distinguishing feature is the fact that power is vested —both theoretically and in practical terms— in all of its members so that decision-making becomes a function of the collective will.

Democracy makes it possible to organize the State on the basis of direct or indirect participatory mechanisms that impart legitimacy to those representing power. According to Plato and Aristotle, there are three forms of social organization: monarchy (rule by one), aristocracy (rule by the best), and democracy (rule by the many). These different forms of government define three distinct kinds of social coexistence, depending on the degree of participation of the organized groups whose presence and consensus afford legitimacy to each structure.

In a democratic State, decisions are made by the people through representatives acting on their behalf and for their benefit. This type of democracy, also known as participatory democracy, allows members of society to organize themselves to influence public decisions when vehicles for popular consultation are provided. In contemporary societies, the most widespread democratic vehicles are those of participatory democracy, the system of government that prevails in most of the world.

The concept of participatory democracy entails direct democratic formulas (public hearings, administrative remedies, among others) to mitigate the merely representative nature of the system.

The separation of powers is the essential feature of representative and participatory democracy as it allows a harmonious coexistence between rulers, lawgivers, and purveyors of justice. This coexistence has as its hallmark the autonomy of, and the respect for, decisions, and the consensual application of those decisions.

The right to elect and to be elected by universal, secret, and direct suffrage is another feature inherent to representative democracies. For this right to be effectively exercised, it is essential that the system allow the existence of political organizations.

This modality of political and social organization requires as a *sine qua non* condition guarantees of freedom of expression for individuals and social groups. Democracy allows everyone to think as he wishes and to express himself as he deems best, within the bounds of the law. This right also encompasses freedom of the press and of the communication channels through which opinions flow in a free exchange of ideas. Lastly, freedom of association is a basic condition of democracy, as it enables individuals and groups to exercise all other democratic freedoms and rights.

Democracy is based on the rule of the majority and full respect for the rights of minorities. However, if abused, majority rule can degenerate into ochlocracy, the tyranny of majority, a patently undemocratic state of affairs. Democratic societies run the risk that the majority may harm the minority with its decisions, thereby negating the very essence of this modality of social and political organization which is government by and for all.

To prevent this kind of democratic degeneration, it is essential that the different branches of the State coexist in harmony, *i.e.*, that they serve as checks and balances on each other and thus prevent dominance by one branch to the detriment of the others.

The independence and separation of powers emerges, therefore, as the very essence of modern representative democracy. Its function is, precisely, to ensure that representation is exercised in harmony and on a level field. Each branch is independent and acts as a constant check to balance the others. This harmonious and balanced situation helps check the acts of all branches and prevent corruption and lawlessness.

Baron Montesquieu, a French *philosophe* and keen observer of society (1689-1755), first conceived of democratic societies as having three separate branches, Executive, Legislative, and Judicial, that served as checks and balances on each other.

The Executive Branch is entrusted with the administration of political power and the promulgation of the laws approved by the Legislative Branch. Executive power is vested in, and represented by, the president of the republic or head of State, elected by popular vote.

The mission of the Legislative Branch is to issue mandatory laws within the framework of the country's constitution. It also monitors the other branches of government. It is the ultimate representation of democratic power, being a collegiate body that reflects the different political tendencies in a society. It is represented by a congress, assembly or parliament elected by the people.

The Judicial Branch is charged with applying the law in accordance with constitutional and statutory provisions in effect in a democratic system. Its main function is to decide and resolve the conflicts that often arise in society. Its independence stands as the guarantee of the impartiality of its legal decisions and judgments. The lack of judicial independence would pose a serious threat to the democratic system.

The justice system in Ecuador

The Judicial Branch in Ecuador suffers from a structural disorder resulting from what prominent sociologist Agustín Cueva used to define as the makeup of power in Ecuador. In his work, Cueva established that Ecuador has been unable to escape populist episodes that have left their imprint in the country's history.

Limiting our scope to recent history, we could begin the story with José María Velasco Ibarra, a markedly populist presence in Ecuadorian politics from the thirties to the seventies of the 20th century. In the 1980s, the Popular Forces Concentration Party led by Asaad Bucaram and Carlos Guevara Moreno before him, gained considerable influence. The nineties witnessed the rise of Abdalá Bucaram, and a young 21st century has already seen the emergence of Lucio Gutiérrez and Rafael Correa, two clearly populist figures.

Ecuador has labored, therefore, under a power structure where the justice system is part of a political game in which the leaders of the day seek to wield power through the unfortunate expedient of using the judiciary for their own purposes.

The great challenge facing Ecuador is succeeding in having an independent, autonomous justice system, removed and free from political games. Most of all, the justice system needs to be extricated from that pernicious power structure that turns it into a political tool.

Ecuador's history proves that the administration of justice was born of, and remained closely tied to, the existing political system of the times.

In October 1821, still during the wars of independence, an Act Organizing Tribunals and Courts established the Superior Court of Justice of Quito (which, nevertheless, sat in Cuenca) as the first step in the creation of a judicial system based on the gradual abolition of slavery, and new reforms aimed at enhancing the economic and political freedoms of the lands of the emerging State. Its doctrinal bases called for the separation of powers, but, in practical terms, the influence of the political system on the Judicial Branch was unavoidable.

Following his victory over Spanish forces at the Battle of Pichincha (May 24, 1822), General Antonio José de Sucre created the first court of justice, the Court of Appeals for the Southern District, in Cuenca. The court was inspired by the Cucuta Constitution of July 1821 that created the State of Gran Colombia[41].

Influence by different constitutions and rulers on the justice system

After Ecuador broke away from Gran Colombia (1830), during the first term of President Juan José Flores (1830-1834), the Judicial Branch continued to develop with the creation of the High Court of Justice of Quito under a provision in the Riobamba Constitution.

The appointment of justices to this court did run into certain difficulties. It was shown that, in actuality, the Legislative and the Executive Branches had taken part in nominating the candidates. This created a precedent for the election of judges along party lines.

The first Ecuadorian Constitution of 1830 not only defined the character of the new republic but also gave the president the power to elect judges from groups of three candidates submitted by the Council of State, a practice that legalized Executive meddling with Judicial Branch matters.

---

41. Gran Colombia included the present-day countries of Colombia, Panama, Venezuela, and Ecuador. It barely lasted 10 years.

Five years later, under the 1835 Constitution, the president of the republic (Vicente Rocafuerte at the time) was empowered to suggest to Congress the names of judicial candidates, thus delegating on the Legislative Branch the responsibility for electing those who would be raised to the bench.

The 1843 Political Charter was issued during President Flores's second term. It again gave the president of the republic the power to select Supreme Court justices.

In 1845, during the provisional government headed by José Joaquín de Olmedo, the National Congress was empowered to choose Supreme Court justices, while the president of the republic continued to appoint Superior Court justices.

Under the 1878 Constitution, during the presidency of Ignacio de Veintemilla, it was provided that justices were to be elected by the National Congress, removing from the president of the republic the responsibility for designating them. Nevertheless, politics continued to intrude into the judicial system.

Similar events occurred during the terms in office of José Plácido Caamaño (1883-1888), Eloy Alfaro (1895-1901 and 1905-1911), Isidro Ayora (1926-1931), José María Velasco Ibarra's second administration (1944-1947), and under President Otto Arosemena Gómez (1966-1968).

The 1978 Constitution, although introducing some minor reforms and transitory provisions, essentially confirmed the political appointment of justices.

9

Changes under the 1998 Constitution

The 1998 Constituent Assembly comprised 70 representatives, two from each province, plus one for each 300,000 inhabitants, elected at large. This ample national representation gave voice to new visions that translated into rights and guarantees that would be incorporated into the new charter.

The new constitution was promulgated on August 10, 1998. For the first time in its history, Ecuador was declared to be a "pluricultural and multiethnic country," and "social market economy" was defined as the model the country would follow.

In the judicial field, the 1998 Constitution emphasized due process as a right of all citizens, to be respected at all levels of the judiciary and by all authorities. Proposals advanced by diverse social groups including indigenous peoples were written into the charter. The office of the People's Ombudsman was enshrined in the constitutional text and several ant-corruption provisions were adopted.

New citizen rights were set forth in Chapter 2 of the Constitution. Chief among them were those related to the right to life and the banning of the death sentence, torture, cruel and unusual punishment, and other similar measures. The rights of citizens to access the media were spelled out.

New threats against the justice system

The Supreme Court of Justice organized in 1997 was the result of a 14-question popular consultation called by Acting President Fabián Alarcón on May 25 of that year. The major issues put to the citizenry were the convening of an Assembly to amend the Constitution, and the authorization to modernize the system for designating Supreme Court Justices.

Ecuadorian voters approved the matters submitted to their consideration in the popular consultation. But the National Congress sitting at the time mocked their vote and decided that "this time, the National Congress shall designate the 31 justices of the Supreme Court of Justice..."

This Court acted until December 20, 2004, when President Lucio Gutiérrez, through Resolution No. R-21-181, decided to "dismiss the justices and their respective associate justices of the Supreme Court of Justice ..." New justices were immediately designated to replace those so cavalierly dispensed with. The new Supreme Court was presided over by Guillermo Castro, widely known in the country by his nickname of "Pichi," which popular wit soon extended to the "Pichi Court" as a whole.

This event proved disastrous for the politicians who rammed it through and was one of the main reasons for President Lucio Gutiérrez's downfall on April 20, 2005. But the damage had already been done, and the justice system emerged from this sad episode broken and discredited.

Hoping to find a way out of this serious problem, the National Congress, with the support of a parliamentary majority comprised of the Social Christian Party (PSC), the Democratic Left (ID), and the indigenous group Pachakutik, approved in mid-2005 several reforms to the Organic Law of the Judicial Branch.

The new statute was accompanied by a new method for selecting Supreme Court justices. A Qualifying Committee was set up, chaired by Carlos Estarellas Merino, which would designate the members of the highest court in Ecuador. The process, which earned wide international acclaim, was monitored by commissions from the Organization of American States (OAS), the United Nations (UN), and the Andean Nations Community (CAN).

In an interview with *Expreso*, a daily newspaper, published on July 12, 2012, Estarellas pointed out the considerable differences that existed between the designation of the "Pichi Court" and the establishment of the 2005 Supreme Court:

> In the first place, there was a difference in the people making the appointments. There was a representative of the various law schools, another of the Superior Courts, a representative of the Anti-Corruption Committee, a representative of the citizenry at large, another representing bar associations. In other words, justices were not designated whimsically. Secondly, and this is an essential point, there were monitoring commissions. The process I presided over was monitored by OAS, UN, and CAN commissions. A monitoring commission that fails to be involved in the process is a blind commission. This was not the case with the Supreme Court designated in 2005. The UN delegate visited the country some six times during the entire process, but delegates

would meet with us every day and were able to observe the process in its entirety. The OAS was represented by [its Secretary General] Jose Miguel Insulza, who came to Ecuador five or six times; and Allan Wagner represented CAN. This is a most significant difference. Third big difference: the Organic Law Reforming the Organic Law of the Judicial Branch set forth the entire process, step by step, and the rules and regulations we drafted covered absolutely everything. These decisions were adopted to avoid subjective decisions, to remove ourselves from the possibility of being pressured. We tried to get politics out of the process and we succeeded. How did we do it? It was simple: anyone who had held political office during the previous five years could not stand as a candidate for a seat in the Supreme Court.

This absolutely transparent process produced the only Supreme Court of Justice that did not result from subjective evaluation criteria or skewed personal interviews, with no meddling of any sort, especially political meddling. The justices so designated were the best qualified, and the Judicial Branch regained its prestige. The process, as the monitors unanimously said it, was an example of transparency for the rest of the world. The excellence of the selection process was reflected in the quality of the opinions and the absence of controversies. And where objections were raised against some of its members, the Supreme Court proceeded to purge itself through a cooptation mechanism that confirmed the absolute transparency of its proceedings and raised it to levels of respectability not seen in Ecuador before or since.

The Court was intended to be a lasting one, but then came the *correísta* onslaught at the Montecristi Constituent Assembly. Veiled pressures were exerted to cause the justices to resign *en masse*, as in fact they did with only a handful of exceptions. The method the government used to bring this about was to pare the number of justices from 31 to 21 and to decide by lots who would stay on the bench and who would leave. This was rightly seen as an insolent and abusive way to deal with individuals who had earned their high office in an absolutely honest and transparent selection process.

The government next proceeded to lower the Supreme Court's status by changing its name to "National Court" and creating a fourth-tier Constitutional Court, hierarchically superior to the no longer supreme "National Court." With that, all the efforts made to institutionalize the highest court in the land wound up in the *correísta* trash bin.

10

The Montecristi Constitution

Early on in his administration, Rafael Correa called a referendum to decide on the convening of a fully empowered Constituent Assembly that would draft a new political charter designed to bring about the changes Ecuadorians expected, including judicial independence. It was an attempt to address civil society's demands, unmet since the fall of President Abdalá Bucaram in 1996. This scenario was further buttressed by memories of the Jamil Mahuad administration (1998-2000), the freezing of the banks accounts of hundreds of thousands of Ecuadorians, the dollarization of the economy, and the subsequent rise and fall of Lucio Gutiérrez, which, taken together with other circumstances, created instability and made the nation lose faith in political organizations.

But to get his Constituent Assembly, Rafael Correa had recourse to an unprecedented political strategy that left the country's institutional order in tatters. The trick was played by his then-minister of the government, Gustavo Larrea.

Former President Gustavo Hurtado recounts the events of those days:

> Once installed in the presidency (and as would happen later whenever he wished to reach a political object be-

yond the pale of the law), he unfoundedly argued that
Article 104 of the Constitution authorized him to consult
the people (... and) chopped off the second part of the
article in question that specifically limited such authority to matters other than constitutional amendments.[42]

Correa submitted his request for a popular consultation to the Supreme Electoral Court (TSE) which, in turn,
forwarded it to Congress for its review. The Legislative
Branch answered by removing Jorge Acosta, chief justice
of the TSE, a move that resulted in the abrupt dismissal of
57 congressmen under a resolution issued by the Electoral
Court[43] accompanied by physical attacks perpetrated by
pro-government goons.

---

42. Osvaldo Hurtado, Dictaduras del siglo XXI: el caso
ecuatoriano [21st-Century Dictatorships: the Ecuadorian Case],
Quito, first edition, Paradiso Editores, p. 59

43. At the time, Rene Maugé was the TSE member representing
the Izquierda Democrática-Red Ética y Democracia alliance. I
was national president of ID and was never consulted on this
TSE decision, as Maugé knew I would never give my consent
to such nonsense. He simply reported the fait accompli after
the decision had already appeared in the media. As soon as I
learned of what had transpired at the TSE, I attempted to contact
Maugé by telephone. He returned my call several hours later.
I told him that resolution was a personal decision of his and
the party did not agree with it. I asked him to resign from his
post, as he had acted outside the party line; he never did. Rene
Maugé currently is a high official in the Correa-controlled National Electoral Council.

That was how, using questionable political maneuvers and naked threats, Rafael Correa imposed his will. The country, hoping for better days, would then be left to approve his request for a Constituent Assembly. The body charged with writing Ecuador's latest political charter began its sessions on November 30, 2007, in the town of Montecristi, Province of Manabí, and concluded its work on July 25, 2008.

The new Constitution incorporated some significant reforms such as jurisdictional guarantees and the principles informing the Judicial Branch. These aspects should have been grouped together but, as a result of the absurd notions of Constituent Assembly members, were instead scattered over the document. These innovations were wholly theoretical and their major flaw was the failure to contribute to judicial independence. In fact, they turned out to be a straitjacket that keeps the Constitution under firm government control.

The Montecristi Constitution introduced changes to the institutional, economic, and social life of the country through the State's control and strategic involvement made possible by a "solidarity-based" economy that replaced the previous "social market economy." It increased executive powers and the president's ability to meddle with economic and currency matters, and provided for one-time immediate reelection, thereby concentrating power in the Executive Branch. In addition, it created a Constitutional Court as the court of last resort, and reduced the number of National Court justices from 31 to 21, a device to control the administration of justice, which is more easily accomplished with a smaller number of judges.

The so-called "actions for protection" replaced the former actions for the protection of constitutional rights, while habeas corpus petitions are no longer heard by mayors but by criminal judges. A novel feature of the Constitution was the recognition of the judicial systems of the various indigenous peoples.

All these changes were made possible by the ample pro-government majority that thoroughly dominated the Constituent Assembly. This one-sided situation permitted the development of a new mechanism for passing bills in block and with no debate.

Deep rifts in the ranks of Alianza PAIS led to the resignation of the Constituent Assembly speaker, Alberto Acosta; he was replaced by Cuenca architect Fernando Cordero, who shepherded the votes necessary for the approval of most constitutional provisions.

The Justice Commission played an important role throughout this process. It insisted on an innovative and *avant-garde* drafting of the dogmatic portion of the new Constitution but neglected the very essence of any charter, its organic provisions. It failed to provide sufficient safeguards to prevent the Judicial Branch from becoming subservient to political power. Ultimately, its work produced poor results, as organic provisions continued to be incompatible with its lofty dogmatic pronouncements. In reality, actual power is wielded from Carondelet Palace, and the judiciary has been used to persecute journalists and political opponents.

Another significant change introduced by the 2008 Constitution was the new definition that transformed Ecuador from "a social state based on the rule of law" into "a constitutional state of rights." The change is enshrined in Article 1 of the Constitution, which provides that "Ecuador is a constitutional state of rights, social, democratic, sovereign, independent, unitary, intercultural, multinational, and lay. It organizes itself as a republic and governs itself in a decentralized manner."

Osvaldo Hurtado has also analyzed the installation of the Constituent Assembly. In his latest book he recalls Correa's symbolic swearing-in ceremony in the village of Zumbahua, a rural area of special significance for the president as he had done his social work stint there as a teacher. At that event, President Hugo Chávez of Venezuela, a guest of Correa's, affirmed that "the constituent assembly was the only peaceful way to refound the republic." Correa added that to do away with the "playdough democracy" that existed in Ecuador it was necessary to control the constituent assembly "with, 60, 70, 80 or 90 per cent of its members." With this statement, the head of the Ecuadorian State showed that his intent was not to reflect political pluralism in the Constituent Assembly but, rather, to impose his voice and his ideology to consolidate his political project but, above all, to build up his own image.[44]

44. Osvaldo Hurtado, Dictaduras del siglo XXI: el caso ecuatoriano [21st-Century Dictatorships: the Ecuadorian Case], Quito, first edition, Paradiso Editores, p. 61

11

A Court with superpowers

Following the approval of the new Constitution, the Judicial Branch consisted of the Constitutional Court, the National Court of Justice, the provincial courts and tribunals, the Council of the Judicature (as the governing body), the Office of the Public Defender and the Office of the Attorney General (both autonomous entities), and the Ministry of Justice, Human Rights, and Worship.

The Supreme Court of Justice became the National Court of Justice and, in one of the more perverse changes, ceased to be the court of last resort. A fourth tier, the Constitutional Court, was created as part of the institutional machinery required to consolidate an authoritarian regime. The new Constitutional Court consist of nine members designated by a qualifying commission made up of two representatives each from the Legislative, Executive, and Transparence and Social Monitoring Branches. These members are selected from candidates vying against each other in an apparent competition subject to monitoring commissions and potential citizen challenges.[45]

45. At the competition recently held to set up this Court, the members of the qualifying commission were clearly identified with correísmo. At the end of the process, they conducted a sort of closed-doors requalification which resulted in a Constitution-

The importance of the Supreme Court of Justice lay in its having been conceived by the 1998 Constitution as an independent entity whose members were designated on the basis of their probity on the bench, in the practice of law, or in their performance in the country's law schools.

But the best evidence that this selection process was a sham is the fact that Patricio Pazmiño,[46] a man with a highly controversial record in several cases,[47] was first re-elected as a justice of the Constitutional Court and subsequently as its chief justice.

As chief justice, he prevailed on the Constitutional Court to order the release of the infamous Floresmilo Villalta, arrested and convicted for raping a minor. In a twisted and obscene feat of judicial legerdemain, he was made the beneficiary of an amnesty decreed by the Montecristi Constituent Assembly and released; his crime against a girl from a very humble family has gone unpunished. The case is a perfect example of *correísmo*'s double moral standards: on the one hand, enshrining the rights of boys and girls in the Constitution, and, on the other,

al Court consisting of justices all of whom are closely linked to the administration.

46. Pazmiño is a loyal correísta yeoman. It is a known fact that he prepared all the documents related to the popular consultation ahead of the Montecristi Constituent Assembly. He had a close personal relationship with the then-minister of the government, Gustavo Larrea, and today is a key man in correísmo.

47. Indeed, several Constitutional Court opinions have toed the government's line, in utter disregard of the Constitution itself and the laws. This clearly compromises the Court's independence and highlights its supine subservience to Carondelet dictates.

leaving them absolutely unprotected simply because it so happens that their rapist is a fellow *correísta* militant.

The same court, presided over by Chief Justice Pazmiño, handed down an opinion establishing that the provisions of the 2008 Constitution were to be retroactively applied. This was done solely to favor the public defender, whose removal had been ordered by the Office of the Comptroller General of the State for being guilty of nepotism, as I reported at the time.[48] Or, to put it differently: they turned the Court into a commissar's office to hear cases of interest to their cronies while ignoring thousands of other matters.

Pazmiño has to live not only under an ethical cloud but is also facing doubts about his academic qualifications. It should be recalled that this man put himself forward as a candidate for Supreme Court justice in 2005 and came in 69th place with a measly score of 44.9/100[49] that kept him off the high court.

But possibly the darkest cloud looming over Pazmiño and his colleagues is their self-designation to the Constitutional Court. Article 25 of the transitional system approved together with the 2008 Constitution in the

48. I proved this allegation in the hearing of my challenge to Pazmiño's designation as justice of the Constitutional Court. As was to be expected, the commission charged with reviewing the challenge, made up in its entirety of allies of correísmo, including the recently appointed member of the Council of the Judicature, Néstor Arbitto, dismissed the challenge.

49. Resolution No. 197, of November 13, 2005, of the Supreme Court Justices and Alternate Justices Qualification, Designation, and Installation Committee.

popular consultation provided that: "Once the new Legislative, Executive, and Transparency and Social Monitoring branches have been constituted, a Qualification Commission shall be established which shall designate the justices and associate justices who shall sit in the first Constitutional Court…" This means that the Court could not be set up until all other branches of the State had been organized. But the former members of the Constitutional Court, acting with bold alacrity, as soon as the present Constitution was promulgated on October 20, 2007, *i.e.*, much before the Executive, the Assembly, and the head of the Transparency Branch were even sworn in, proceed by stealth, through the backdoor as it were, to designate themselves as the first Constitutional Court so as to continue enjoying their positions and helping make possible the abuses and outrages of *correísmo* with lamentable opinions favorable to the regime and injurious to the interests of society at large.

This development was of enormous importance, as it is within the Constitutional Court's purview to hear and decide public actions for declarations of unconstitutionality, whether on the grounds of form or substance; *sua sponte*, to declare unconstitutional any related statutes; at the request of the party concerned, to hear and rule on the unconstitutionality of the administrative acts of any public authority; at the request of the party concerned, to hear and rule on actions filed to guarantee the constitutional application of statutes or administrative acts of a general nature; to issue precedent-setting opinions in actions for the protection of constitutional rights, habeas corpus, habeas data, access to public information, and all other constitutional proceedings, and in cases submitted to it for review; to decide conflicts of jurisdiction or attributions between branches of the State or organs established under the Constitution; *sua sponte*, to immediately monitor the constitutionality of declarations of states of emergency whenever they should imply the suspension of constitutional rights; to hear and punish the failure to comply with constitutional judgments and opinions; to declare the unconstitutionality of acts by State institutions or public authorities who should fail to observe, in whole or in part, any constitutional provisions. As can be seen, it is an organ endowed with enormous and transcendental powers that turn it into the perfect tool to support and maintain an autocratic regime.

The present National Court of Justice

It does the people little good to have a prolix description of its rights if those rights and guarantees are not duly observed and applied. No one really cares about all the ink used in praise of due process if, at the time of trial, its provisions are violated. Theoretical rights are one thing, but what really matters is the actual implementation of those rights. The former belong in the dogmatic part of the Constitution, which is unassailable; the latter is a function of the organic part of the Constitution, which reflects the working of institutions.

Turning the Constitutional Court into the highest court in the land is not appropriate. Even less appropriate is to assign to it the power to interpret the Constitution, for it is more a political than a jurisdictional body. The Supreme (National) Court of Justice ought to be the court of last resort, as it is in most civilized countries in the world.

Under the Montecristi Constitution, the National Court of Justice consists of 21 justices, appointed for nine-year terms and sitting in specialized divisions. It is presided over by the chief justice, who holds his position for three years. The National Court remains in Quito.

The functions of the National Court are described in Article 184 of the Constitution: hearing motions to vacate, to review, and all others established by law; developing a system of jurisprudential precedents based on thrice-issued opinions; hearing cases brought against public servants enjoying special jurisdictional privileges; introducing bills related to the justice administration system.

It bears pointing out that the procedures established in the 2008 Constitution for the selection and designation of National Court justices did not do away with the flaws of the old politicized, partial, and, therefore, inefficient system.

Undoubtedly, politicized institutions such as the courts of justice, where the doctrinal precepts of the Political Charter are given short shrift, are partly to blame for the dramatic situation Ecuador finds itself in. The fact of the matter is that, from a dogmatic standpoint, we indulge in parliamentary lyricism, but, in practice, all those principles are prosaically subverted and discretionally applied..

12

A made-in-Venezuela franchise

Correísmo has invented nothing. In fact, its political project is a carbon copy of the Hugo Chávez model in Venezuela. Evidence of this is the fact that Rafael Correa has followed in the steps of the self-appointed Bolivian leader and reproduced his franchise with singular alacrity.

Both presidents — Rafael Correa and Hugo Chávez — took advantage of a favorable situation in their respective countries to translate their fellow citizens's bitter disappointment into votes. Both came to power democratically, using the same discourse: the deterioration of traditional political parties. They deftly used existing electoral rules guaranteeing transparent elections only to later turn them into birds of prey let loose on their adversaries and enlisted in support of their own evil purposes.

Immediately after assuming power, both Chávez and Correa convened a constituent assembly. In fact, the mechanism was identical: a simple executive decree and the rubber-stamping of a statute.

As was to be expected, both constituent assemblies were "fully empowered" so as to claim all State functions. With rather indecent haste, they proceeded to the systematic dismantling of their countries' institutions. And they both relied on the same advisor, Roberto Viciano, especially invited from Spain for the drafting of the new constitutions.

And once the term set for the constituent bodies ended, a legislative commission came into being in both Venezuela and Ecuador that was nothing more than a continuation of the respective Constituent Assemblies and equally subject to the dictates of the Executive Branch. Under the umbrella provided by this sort of assembly, both countries reorganized courts, tribunals, and even notary offices, filling them —of course— with government creatures. Official discourse explained that such restructuring was made necessary by the decay and corruption afflicting the judicial system. In truth, the only goal was total control over all State institutions, ensuring that nothing and no one was left beyond the reach of the long arm of the government.

Both constitutions made it clear that the countries' national project revolved around one single individual: the president of the republic. Laws and regulations were issued to heap even more powers on the Executive Branch.

And then the political consolidation of the new order got underway. The first step was to weaken labor unions. In Ecuador, this was accomplished through the issuance of "Constituent Mandates" first, followed by the repeal of the Organic Law of the Civil Service and Administrative Career (LOSCCA), and the approval of the Organic Law of the Public Service (LOSEP).

Great importance was attached to revenue enhancement. Taxes had to go up, mostly to maintain subsidies and bonuses. Exchange controls and hefty import tariffs were imposed. Both models are identical although, in Venezuela's case, more extreme controls had to be implemented as a result of the meteoric depreciation of the country's currency.

The last step in this Venezuelan "franchise" is the approval of presidential reelection. It should be recalled that Chávez had no qualms in amending his own tailor-made constitution to prolong his mandate at a point when his health clearly prevented him for serving out his term. But, nothing daunted, his acolytes overcame the constitutional requirement of his swearing-in with a highly controversial construction of the law. It should come as no surprise, therefore, that those seated at the banquet table in Carondelet Palace are already plotting a similar maneuver in the event that Correa should be reelected in the next elections.

13

Rafael Correa or
narcissistic Stalinism

Rafael Correa believes himself a monarch and acts like one. He decries democratic institutions to the point of having publicly declared that, as president of the republic, he was also the head of all branches of government.[50] Indeed, he has gone after, and secured, total control over all branches of government in a clear expression of his rejection of the institutional order and an already precarious democratic culture.

Before being elected president, Correa had never been involved in party politics or won an election, except to the student body in college. He was not a politician; he never took part in social movements or anything of the sort. The only high political office he held — for three months— was the ministry of finances. His record — or, more accurately, his lack thereof— probably helps explain his failure to understand the value of political parties and democratic institutions. Betraying his initial promises, he has fostered the dismantling of the State's institutions at a time when, in the wake of a cycle of political instability, what the country needed was precisely a strengthening of those institutions. This has not happened by accident; it

---

50. The source for this extraordinary statement is given elsewhere in this chapter.

is the result of a deliberate plan for the razing of national institutions conceived in the clear understanding that an authoritarian government cannot survive or remain in power if the country's institutions are robust. *Correísmo*'s sinister plan has been systematically carried out and institutions have been hollowed out from the inside, left as empty shells bearing equally empty names. They have become mere puppets whose strings are being pulled from the president's office by a man who believes the country's history began with him, as the past —and he firmly believes this— is of no value or significance. Correa is persuaded that the history of Ecuador began with him and its destiny is indissolubly linked to his own existence, to his vision, and, of course, to the officious opinions of the Venezuelan leader.

His government, admittedly quite efficient in demolishing institutions, has ignored the separation of powers with the connivance, it must be said, of some academics now in the government's payroll who in the past had taken positions at daggers drawn with the notions they now defend. Correa has inveighed against his opponents, has insulted (Exhibit 26)[51] anyone who dares disagree with him and fails to repeat his utterances as holy writ. He has magnified his diatribes through an impressive propaganda machine that floods all media in an attempt to impose his opinion as the sole and irrefutable truth, an opinion based on his singular interpretation of facts doctored as

---

51. Attached is a list of the insults hurled by Correa in his notorious Saturday nationwide broadcasts. I read out this list during a session of the National Assembly. There is nothing else left to say.

circumstances require and tampered with until they fit his interests.

That such lurches are so blatant as to constitute an insult to the intelligence of Ecuadorians is a consideration that fails to move the president. Thus, Correa's favorite cousin, a man who until yesterday had been "hounded" by a "corrupt press" and the victim of a "media lynching," is now a traitor who must be called back to account, not only to the courts but first and foremost to His Majesty, for his manifold lies and forgeries that have laid low the leader's credibility.

Simón Pachano[52] has masterfully described the situation:

> There is an historic precedent that shows this is a feature shared by leaders foreordained to change the world. Stalin, the Father of All the Russias, kept his own cowed followers in suspense. The truth of the day was kept from them. They would go to bed in the shadow of the Molotov-Ribbentrop Pact and would wake up in the midst of a a Great Patriotic War against that scourge of the working classes, the Nazi party. In the morning they would sing the praises of Kamenev and Zinoviev until they learned in the evening that they should be denounced and their deaths demanded because they had always been traitors. They despised European social democrats, but only until the day they became the USSR's historic allies. The true truth came from the word of the leader, and he who did not believe in it would be consigned to darkness (oftentimes the ultimate darkness of death).

52. An editorial published in *El Universo* on January 7, 2013, p. 6

The same propaganda machinery has been engaged to promote the president's personality cult and appropriate Ecuadorians' national and historic symbols. The president claims for himself the triumphs of the great Eloy Alfaro, whose equal he professes to be. In a desperate move to cloak himself in the liberal caudillo's mantle, he absurdly promoted the Old Fighter (in his grave for 100 years) to general, even though that promotion had been conferred almost one century earlier. He has unashamedly taken over and politically claimed for himself the lyrics of songs such as *Patria, tierra sagrada*, and has carried the ashes of illustrious Ecuadorians in pompous processions around the country.

So large is his vanity and so scant his political culture that his mistakes have caused Ecuador no small degree of international embarrassment.

A harbinger of things to come occurred on June 27, 2007, when he called journalist Sandra Ochoa "a horrid fat woman," supposedly for having addressed him "in an absolutely ill-bred manner." Sandra Ochoa is a journalist from Cuenca, the recipient of several national and international awards. This ungentlemanly insult was the first shot in what would prove to be a constant barrage of invective against journalists and the media.

In March 2009, during one of his Saturday nationwide broadcasts, Rafael Correa made one of the most controversial statements of his mandate. Speaking of his meddling with the State, he said:

...the president of the Republic, and listen to me and listen well, is not only the head of the Executive Branch; he is the head of the entire Ecuadorian state, and the

Ecuadorian state is the Executive Branch, the Legislative Branch, the Judicial Branch, the Electoral Branch, the Transparency and Social Control Branch, the offices of the superintendents, the attorney general, the comptroller – all that is the Ecuadorian state."

This extraordinary declaration revealed Correa's innermost convictions. And that is, beyond any doubt, the manner in which he has governed the country.

Correa is in the habit of insulting not only his domestic opponents but also his foreign critics or, simply, any individual abroad who does not share his thinking. In early December 2009, then-Colombian Defense Minister Juan Manuel Santos published a book with details of the military operation of March 1, 2008, that destroyed the military camp of the F.A.R.C. guerrilla leader known as Raúl Reyes. The raid took place in Angostura, on Ecuadorian territory. The book so irked Correa that his reaction was to speak of the now president of Colombia in the following terms:

> That poor man has got a shoe for a brain and a stone for a heart. We would be happy to talk about him, but we're not going to help him sell his pathetic book; it isn't worth the effort.

In late August 2012, when 72 people attempting to cross the border into the United States were murdered in Tamaulipas, Mexico, there were two survivors of the massacre, an Ecuadorian and a Honduran. President Correa reported the crime with these words: "What happened last week in Mexico is unspeakable. May I take advantage of this opportunity to let you know that our brother Freddy Lala (the Ecuadorian survivor) is already safe and sound in our country." Correa added that Lala was the person who "broke the news of the mass killings and led the authorities to the scene of this atrocious crime." Finally, the head of the Ecuadorian State explained that Lala "tells us there was another survivor whom we do not wish to put in jeopardy: a Honduran citizen." These statements triggered controversies in Honduras and Ecuador. Honduran authorities and Ecuadorian human rights organizations felt that Correa had acted imprudently in disclosing information that could endanger the lives of both men. Honduras Foreign Minister Mario Canahuati called Correa "irresponsible." Correa lashed back: "… here comes this insolent chancellor of the illegitimate government of Honduras [...] saying that President Correa is irresponsible. I'm not going to waste my time answering idiotic statements."

He cast another of his peerless pearls during the nationwide broadcast on Saturday January 7, 2012, when he referred to a New Year's party held at Carondelet Palace. Correa waxed lyrical in exalting the beauty of his female coreligionists:

> I don't know whether gender equality makes democracy better. But there can be no doubt it has improved the fun [...] Some beautiful Assemblywomen we've got! *Corcho* [addressing Fernando Cordero, speaker of the National Assembly and a member of Alianza PAIS by his nickname], we've got to raise their salaries. Look at them, the poor things. They had no money to buy

enough material and are all in miniskirts ... Oh, my God! [...] I was told their legs are simply spectacular.

Not even U.S. President Barack Obama could escape Correa's insults and embarrassing comments. On May 3, 2012, speaking during the commemoration of the International Day of Freedom of the Press, Obama referred to the "threats and harassment" directed in Ecuador against journalist César Ricaurte, the founder of Fundamedios, an NOG. A few weeks earlier, Ricaurte had gone before the Inter-American Commission on Human Rights (IACHR) to denounce alleged attacks against freedom of the press in his country. On May 5, in his customary nationwide broadcast, Correa responded. "We know the United States has always protected its informants, but to have President Obama himself come out to defend them is a disgrace. [...] What do they think? Who do they think they are talking to? They are talking to the government of the "citizen revolution" and we'll have them respect the country's sovereignty [...] That's why he squares the circle so neatly, that's why Fundamedios and Ricaurte have had access to Washington and to the Inter-American Commission on Human Rights. Of course ... birds of a feather flock together."

While admitting Australian hacker Julian Assange's great skills as a communicator — and, as corollary, his evident limitations in the field of law —, Correa attempted to justify the crimes Assange might have committed in Sweden. On August 26, 2013, news agency AFP highlighted an interview Correa gave the British *Sunday Times* in which he defended his granting of asylum to the Wikileaks founder. When asked whether he did not think that forcing oneself on a woman was a crime, the Ecuadorian president answered:

> The woman he was with? Both sleeping on the same bed? Let's leave this to the Swedish judicial system. To give you an example, not using a condom when having sex is not a crime in Latin America." Correa added: "the crimes Assange is being charged with would not be criminal acts in 90 or 95 per cent of the planet.

On December 5, 2013, during an interview he granted Argentine TV channel C5N, Correa was asked about the Iranian government's refusal to hand over to Argentine justice several officials wanted for the bombing of the Association of Argentine Mutual Assistance Jewish Organizations (AMIA). He replied: "I am familiar with the case. It is very painful for Argentine history. But look at how many people were killed by the NATO bombings of Libya. Let's compare things and see where the true dangers lie; let's not engage in manipulations." Correa's words angered the Jewish community in Argentina, whose government demanded an apology from the Ecuadorian president. Days later, during a conversation with the Ecuadorian ambassador to Argentina, picked up by several media outlets, Correa said: "I don't feel I need to apologize. I don't think I've insulted anyone, and I'm not going to apologize for something I don't feel guilty of."

This clearly shows that Correa is not, by far, a man of the left or, even less, a socialist. Historically, from classical socialism to the most diverse versions of social democracy, socialist thought has defended freedom. And any abridgement of freedom is incompatible with any form of social-ism. Anyone attempting to muzzle the press, to set up an institutional mirage for the purpose of consolidating his authoritarian rule; anyone ignoring the division of powers and trampling them underfoot; anyone who engages in *ad hominem* attacks against his opponents and systematically persecutes them; anyone who thrives in the cult of his own personality, who mistakes tyranny for strength, who up-holds his followers' misdeeds and inveighs against those who denounce them; anyone who imposes fear instead of fostering peace; anyone who divides and confronts and declares himself the enemy of consensus and agreement; anyone, finally, who betrays his pledged word and is drunk with power, can be anything but a man of the left or, much less, a socialist.

It being impossible to pigeonhole *correísmo* within the spectrum of political options, it becomes necessary to have recourse to a rather apt description. Correa's government is the rule of narcissistic Stalinism.

Rafael Correa's figures

In January 2007, Ecuadorians clearly understood that the major issues the new Correa administration had to tack-le were corruption and unemployment. Ecuador had just gone through a long period of corruption scandals that began in 1996 during the government of President Abdalá Bucaram with high-profile cases like the so-called "school bookbag" case. It continued with the banking collapse during Jamil Mahuad's term, and concluded with the sad and laughable episode of the "Pichi Court" that led to the fall of President Lucio Gutiérrez.

According to *Market*, a public opinion polling company, in January 2007 28% of Ecuadorians believed corruption to be the country's most pressing problem; 29% believed it was unemployment.[53]

After six years of *correísmo*, the figures have changed. Although unemployment continues to be a pressing problem for many Ecuadorians, crime and insecurity are now the major concern of 48% of respondents; unemployment is mentioned by only 18%.[54]

This means that although people have the perception that the economy has improved and the country has regained stability (thanks to high oil prices and higher taxes), citizen insecurity has increased alarmingly.

Rafael Correa's six years have been a tale of inefficiency when it comes to tackling citizen insecurity, an issue intimately related to the justice system. In a country where, according U.N. Special Rapporteur on Extrajudicial Executions Philip Alston, barely 1.3% of all deaths reported to the police result in an adjudication of guilt, the doors are open to criminals to continue terrorizing society.

This issue, plus the never-ending cases of corruption and the problems facing the country's economy, have worn down Rafael Correa's image.

Market has made an historic analysis of the president's popularity numbers. It shows that it has been at times when he was receiving his lowest scores that he decided to call for a popular consultation.

---

53. Market, "Situación actual del Ecuador" ["Ecuador's present situation"], November 2012

54. Ibid

It can be said, therefore, that the popular consultation and referendum was a political card the president played at one of his administration's more unpopular junctures to try to address the problem of insecurity, one of the most pressing issues facing Ecuador.

The president's move did not turn out as well as he had hoped. By the time the popular consultation and referendum was held, on May 7, 2011, his popularity had plunged again, this time to an all-time low of 36%.[55]

---

55. Ibid.

14

The New Judicature

The appointment of the new Council of the Judicature is a clear indication that *correísmo* is completing its takeover of the justice system. Former minister and Correa's private secretary, Gustavo Jalkh, became chairman of the Council, the other four members of which are unconditional Correa loyalists. Tania Arias and Paulo Rodríguez had already proved their usefulness in the Transitional Council of the Judicature, while Néstor Arbitto is a former minister of justice under Correa, and Ana Karina Peralta had worked for Jalkh and for Fernando Alvarado in the National Communications Department.

But irregularities actually go back to the appointment of the monitors who would supervise the process. A total of 77 people were accredited to discharge this duty. Accreditation was entrusted to the Transparency and Social Monitoring Council, an entity controlled by its *correísta* majority, as previously noted. The hardly surprising outcome was that at least six monitors were card-carrying members of the government movement, according to Alianza PAIS records.[56]

---

56. They are Ana Miranda (Guayas), Jesús Nagua (El Oro), Rosa Vásquez, Gaden Rosales, and Byron Analuza (Pichincha), and Bismarck Vélez (Manabí). "Hay militantes de AP en veeduría

The rules and regulations governing the creation of monitoring commissions for selecting citizen commissions and designating authorities did not prohibit the participation of members of political organizations. However, monitors were banned from "tying the monitoring commission to personal, group or party interests, and pursuing electoral purposes."

But since cynicism and audacity are boundless in the days of the "citizen revolution", even the coordinator of this citizen branch was closely identified with the Correa government. Luis Quishpi, chairman of the Artisans Defense Board is the president's direct delegate to the monitoring commission.

Skepticism over the new justice system

Writing in the internet portal *Línea de Fuego* [*Firing Line*] on August 28, 2012, renowned jurist Mario Melo described popular skepticism over this process led and conducted by the "citizen revolution". By way of conclusion, Melo points out that "... the political capital invested by the regime in changing the justice system must necessarily be linked to an effective commitment to guarantees that judicial proceedings are not only timelier, conducted in more modern and functional scenarios, and by revamped judicial personnel, but, above all, that it generates in the citizenry confidence that decisions will be made according to law, to rights, and to justice, without fears and without favoring the political power."

---

de la Judicatura" ["AP militants in the Judicature's monitoring commission"], El Universo, November 20, 2012

Melo states that the weak point of this judicial reform lies precisely in the designation of judicial officials with no political commitments that would tie their hands. One of the more controversial issues, he adds, was the designation of the new members of the National Court of Justice. "Complaints have not been long in coming, and one of the arenas where they have been heard is the International Monitoring Commission under Baltasar Garzón, established by the Citizen Participation Council and the Ministry of Justice. The Commission's First Preliminary Report contains the complaints filed by Assembly Member Andrés Páez against the grades assigned to judges Wilson Merino, Mariana Yumbay, and Lucy Blacio, who appear to have received scores inconsistent with their qualifications as otherwise determined in the competition ..."

The fact of the matter is that the judicial system found itself embroiled in controversy over a series of events. In the first place, the International Monitoring Commission's report stupefied CJT members who had assiduously wined and dined the monitors. Then came the National Court of Justice's lukewarm response: in declining to purge itself, it besmirched the reputation of justices legitimately selected. This was followed by the admission and flight of Correa's cousin, the infamous Pedro Delgado, which nevertheless failed to bestir the Office of the Attorney General into action, even though it had earlier displayed great prosecutorial zeal in the "Luluncoto Ten" and "September 30" cases; in fact, Delgado, a confessed criminal, was allowed to flee to Miami on a first-class commercial flight. The Citizen Participation Council's decision to set up a monitoring commission to review the work done by the International

Monitoring Commission (Exhibit 29) came next, a move that was met with widespread indignation and derision. And then the Office of the Attorney General, apparently suffering from congenital ineptitude, made the latest in a long line of blunders: it closed the notorious "drug suitcase" case and tacitly declared that the drugs made their way into the Chancery under their own power: they got themselves into packages, they affixed the diplomatic seals themselves, and they traveled to Italy without assistance from any human agency. The drugs, the Attorney General helpfully clarified, managed to get themselves across the border because the dogs' sense of smell happened to be off that day. And to top it all off, the Attorney General himself now asked for the arrest of Pedro Delgado, allowed to flee the country a few days earlier after admitting having forged his economics degree. Delgado was guilty of either ideological falsehood or of the fraudulent use of documents, as he had parlayed his forged decree into high offices bestowed upon him by his first cousin, President Correa. Around that same time, Tania Arias made the categorical pronouncement that the appointments to the National Court of Justice were a "closed case." And lastly, the new Council of the Judicature was packed with members who are clearly creatures of Correa and the government.

These developments, revealing as they do the profound rot in the administration of justice in Ecuador and *correísmo's* "messing" with it, have elicited a deep sense of frustration and skepticism in the nation. Ecuadorians have seen with their own eyes that the much-vaunted "ethical pillars" of the "citizen revolution" were toppled a long time ago..

So, what do we do now?

We Ecuadorians do not have to put up with these abuses of power, with overweening pride, with constitutional and legal violations justified with the pretext of new roads and infrastructure (which, incidentally, were paid for with taxpayer's money); in politics, doing one's duty is expected and earns no merits. Our duty is to continue fighting these proven cases of corruption.

As I write the closing lines of this book, the National Court of Justice has published over the signatures of fewer than half of its members (only 13 justices, including the controversial Paúl Íñiguez) a timid public communiqué washing their hands and declining the recommendation of the International Monitoring Commission that the Court proceed to purge itself. The Court, the signing minority argued, did not appoint the justices being challenged. So, the ball was now in the Council of the Judicature's court, but the Council limited itself to claiming for the nth time, and in the face of overwhelming evidence to the contrary, that the justices were designated in a "transparent" manner.

The National Court is thus allowing illegitimate justices to continue issuing equally illegitimate orders and rulings. In the future, any party harmed by such illegitimate decisions will not hesitate in appealing to international courts. And, on the basis of the International Monitoring Commission's report, international tribunals will have more than sufficient grounds to overturn those decisions and order substantial damages that, once more, will have to be paid with monies belonging to all Ecuadorians.

Illegitimate judges taint their decisions with their illegitimacy. Other National Court justices must address this very serious situation if they do not wish their own orders and opinions to come under a pall of doubt. Those other justices are legitimate as they were selected on the basis of their qualifications, but their standing is being sullied by failed candidates masquerading as justices. They are aware of the situation, as is indeed the chief justice of the National Court of Justice. They cannot afford to remain inactive. The longer they allow this situation to continue, the more serious the damages to their legitimate performance will be.

www.jueceschimbos.com: The right to resistance

The right to resistance is not a fabrication of the opposition. It was enshrined in Article 98 of the Constitution by the intellectual father of the charter. Article 98 provides:

> Individuals and groups may exercise the right of resistance against actions or omissions of the public power or of non-State physical or legal persons which violate or may violate their constitutional rights, and demand the acknowledgment of new rights.

The grounds for invoking the right to resistance are therefore clearly set forth in the Constitution. There have been actions and omissions by the Transitional Council of the Judicature that have effectively violated the rights of candidates who, although having better qualifications and higher scores, were deliberately harmed and excluded from the National Court of Justice. The principles of judicial independence and autonomy have been flagrantly violated.

Collective rights such as the right of all Ecuadorians to be tried by impartial, independent, and neutral courts, not tainted by political influences, have been violated. Constitutional and statutory provisions, rules and regulations have been violated. Procedures have been infringed. Subjective mechanisms, incompatible with the transparency required of a selection process, have been applied.

There are more than sufficient grounds, therefore, for all of us to invoke the right to resistance and to not abide by the results of the actions of the notorious triumvirate in the Transitional Council of the Judicature. The orders and opinions of illegitimate justices are clearly tainted and suffer from manifest flaws, as they are being issued by individuals who are not empowered to sit as national justices.

To facilitate the exercise of this right, I have made available to all citizens the webpage www.jueceschimbos.com, to collect complaints against the doings of these illegitimate justices and failed candidates whose top qualification is to be militant *correístas*.

The objective conditions for the exercise of these actions already exist. All that is needed is for people to make up their minds and do what the Paris students did in 1968, what Nelson Mandela did in his historic struggle against racism, what Martin Luther King did in his memorable defense of the civil rights of minorities, what peoples all over the world have done in their fight against tyrants: *Not Be Afraid..*

Exhibits

Exhibit 1

Exhibit 2

Exhibit 3

Exhibit 4

EL CONSEJO DE LA JUDICATURA DE TRANSICIÓN

RESOLUCIÓN No. 007-2011

CONSIDERANDO:

Que, el Código Orgánico de la Función Judicial, en el artículo 264 numeral 1, otorga al Pleno del Consejo de la Judicatura, entre otras, la función de nombrar y evaluar a las juezas y jueces y a las conjuezas y a los conjueces de la Corte Nacional de Justicia.

Que, mediante resolución número 006-2011, de 19 de agosto de 2011 el Pleno del Consejo de la Judicatura aprobó el Reglamento de concursos de méritos y oposición, impugnación ciudadana y control social para la selección y designación de servidoras y servidores de la Función Judicial.

Que, el artículo 1 del antes citado Reglamento, establece que el Pleno del Consejo de la Judicatura aprobará los respectivos instructivos para los concursos de méritos y oposición que se convoquen de conformidad con el Código Orgánico de la Función Judicial y este Reglamento.

En ejercicio de la atribución prevista en el artículo 264, numeral 10, del Código Orgánico de la Función Judicial expide el:

INSTRUCTIVO PARA EL CONCURSO DE MÉRITOS Y OPOSICIÓN, IMPUGNACIÓN CIUDADANA Y CONTROL SOCIAL, PARA LA SELECCIÓN Y DESIGNACIÓN DE JUEZAS Y JUECES DE LA CORTE NACIONAL DE JUSTICIA

Exhibit 5

Actividades Desarrolladas

Regresar

Información General del Juicio:

No. Causa: 2012-0401
Judicatura: JUZGADO DECIMO SEGUNDO DE LO CIVIL
Accion/Delito: CONFESION JUDICIAL
Actor/Ofendido: PAEZ BENALCAZAR ANDRES TARQUINO
Demandado/Imputado: DRA. MARIANA YUMBAY YALLICO
Sorteos Segunda Instancia:

Detalle de Actividades:

No.	Fecha	Actividad
1	2012-04-24	**ACTA GENERAL** RECIBIDO HOY VEINTE Y OCHO DE MARZO DEL DOS MIL DOCE, A LAS DIECISEIS HORAS CON TREINTA MINUTOS, CON SOBRE CERRADO.- CERTIFICO. DR. FERNANDO NARANJO FACTOS. SECRETARIO. RAZON.- SIENTO POR TAL QUE COPIA DE LA PRESENTE DEMANDA LA AGREGO AL LIBRO COPIADOR DE DEMANDAS QUE MANTIENE LA JUDICATURA.- QUITO, 28 DE MARZO DEL 2012.- CERTIFICO.- DR. FERNANDO NARANJO FACTOS. SECRETARIO.

Exhibit 6

Exhibit 7

RESULTADO ESTADO TRIBUTARIO

Fecha: 26/06/20

SRì
...te hace bien al país!

RUC: 0702604901801   MERINO SANCHEZ WILSON YOVANNY

Estado Tributario: AL DIA EN SUS OBLIGACIONES

Permiso Facturación:	TOTAL 12 MESES	Proceso: DIARIO	14/05/2012 23:55:07
Estado:	ACTIVO	Declarante: SI	Ubicado: SI

Tipo Persona: PERSONA NATURAL
Clase Contribuyente: OTROS
Fecha Notificación: Fecha Baja:

Fecha Inicio Actividad: 20/10/1993   Fecha Actualización: 10/01/2012
Fecha Liquidación: 29/07/1999   Fecha Reinicio: 29/07/1999

Exhibit 8

Actividades Desarrolladas

Regresar

Información General del Juicio:

No. Causa: 2012-0392
Judicatura: JUZGADO VIGESIMO QUINTO DE LO CIVIL
Accion/Delito: CONFESION JUDICIAL
Actor/Ofendido: DR. ANDRES TARQUINO PAEZ BENALCAZAR
Demandado/Imputado: DR. WILSON MERINO SANCHEZ
Sorteos Segunda -
Instancia: _

Detalle de Actividades:

No.	Fecha	Actividad
1	2012-04-02	RAZON Presentado el veinte y ocho de marzo del dos mil doce a las dieciseis horas cuarenta minutos, un sobre cerrado .-Certifico. DR. LUIS FERNANDO SERRANO SECRETARIO RAZÓN.- En esta fecha deje copia de la demanda que antecede en el archivo de esta judicatura .- Quito, 28 de marzo del 2012 .- Certifico.- DR. LUIS FERNANDO SERRANO SECRETARIO

Exhibit 9

 ASAMBLEA CONSTITUYENTE REPÚBLICA DEL ECUADOR

ACCIÓN DE PERSONAL

Fecha: junio 16 de 2008

VINTIMILLA MOSCOSO	MARÍA XIMENA
APELLIDOS	NOMBRES
102793031	06 de junio de 2008
No. de Cédula de Ciudadanía	Rige a partir de:

FRANCISCO TORRES BUENO
DIRECTOR GENERAL ADMINISTRATIVO DE LA ASAMBLEA CONSTITUYENTE

CONSIDERANDO:

Lo dispuesto en los Arts. 16, 64, 65 y 66 del Reglamento de Funcionamiento de la Asamblea Constituyente y la delegación de funciones emitida el 14 de diciembre del 2007 por la Comisión Directiva;

RESUELVE:

Dar por terminada la relación laboral con la Dra. María Ximena Vintimilla Moscoso – Asesora 1 de la Asambleísta Rosana Alvarado Carrión; por renuncia voluntaria, de conformidad con el Art. 64 inciso tercero del Reglamento de funcionamiento de la Asamblea Constituyente, Oficio S/N de fecha 05 de junio de 2008 suscrito por la interesada, y Oficio RAC-CI032-08 de fecha 11 de junio de 2008.

SITUACIÓN ACTUAL

Unidad: Despacho de Asambleísta

Puesto: ASESORA 1

Lugar de Trabajo: Montecristi – Manabí

Remuneración Mensual Unificada: $3,200.00

Ángel Torres Moncayo
DIRECTOR DE RECURSOS HUMANOS

Francisco Torres Bueno
DIRECTOR GENERAL ADMINISTRATIVO

Registro y control de nómina

Nº: 000520   **Fecha:** 1 6 JUN 2008   f.) Responsable del registro

CÓDIGO: DEP-RRHH-0008

DOY FE: Que la FOTOCOPIA que antecede en ... foja ... es igual al original que se presentó para su evidencia ...
Cuenca, a ... de ... de 2011

Dr. Francisco Carrasco Vintimilla   MONTECRISTI - MANABÍ
Notaría Quinto - Cantón Cuenca

Exhibit 10

ACCION DE PERSONAL:

No. 000930-A

FECHA:

* REPUBLICA DEL ECUADOR

Ministerio
de Relaciones Exteriores,
Comercio e Integración

APELLIDOS:	NOMBRES:
VINTIMILLA MOSCOSO	MARIA XIMENA

No. CEDULA CIUDADANA:	No. CEDULA VOTACION:	RIGE A PARTIR DE:
01027930031		20-Jul-09

EXPLICACION:

En virtud de la Acción de Personal N°1470-DRH-FGE, de 20 de julio del 2009, con la que el doctor Washington Pesántez Muñoz, Fiscal General del Estado, declara en Comisión de Servicios sin remuneración a la doctora María Ximena Vintimilla Moscoso, con la presente Acción de Personal se le nombra como Asesora del señor Ministro de Relaciones Exteriores, Comercio e Integración, a partir del 20 de julio de 2009.

INGRESO	X	SUBROGACION		RENUNCIA	
ASCENSO		ENCARGO ADM.		SUPRESION DE PUESTO	
TRASLADO		COMISION DE SERVICIOS		DESTITUCION	
ROTACION		REVALORIZACION		JUBILACION	
VACACIONES		RECLASIFICACION		SANCION DISCIPLINARIA	
LICENCIAS		NOMBRAMIENTO PROV.		OTROS	

SITUACION ACTUAL	SITUACION PROPUESTA
UNIDAD ADMINISTRATIVA:	UNIDAD ADMINISTRATIVA:
PUESTO:	PUESTO: Asesoría
CATEGORIA:	CATEGORIA: Asesor 2
LUGAR DE TRABAJO:	LUGAR DE TRABAJO: QUITO
REMUNERACION MENSUAL:	REMUNERACION MENSUAL: $ 3,240.00
No. PARTIDA PRESUPUESTARIA:	No. PARTIDA PRESUPUESTARIA:
	2009120020000/0010000002 1AH91031020030008100000000 110

REGISTRO Y CONTROL	
Responsable del Registro Recursos Humanos	Dr. Fander Falconí B. Ministro de Relaciones Exteriores, Comercio e Integración

CONSEJO DE LA JUDICATURA DE TRANSICION
DIRECCION NACIONAL DE PERSONAL
CERTIFICA QUE EL DOCUMENTO ES LA COPIA LA DE
LA COPIA QUE REPOSA EN LA CARPETA PERSO
FECHA: 01/02/12
FIRMA: C.

Exhibit 11

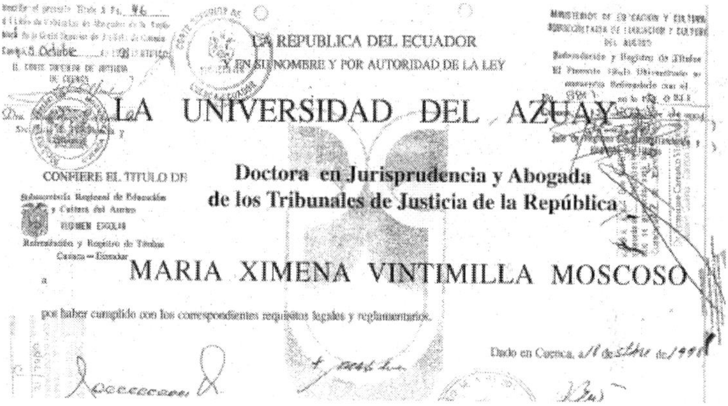

LA REPUBLICA DEL ECUADOR
Y EN SU NOMBRE Y POR AUTORIDAD DE LA LEY

LA UNIVERSIDAD DEL AZUAY

CONFIERE EL TITULO DE **Doctora en Jurisprudencia y Abogada**
de los Tribunales de Justicia de la República

a **MARIA XIMENA VINTIMILLA MOSCOSO**

por haber cumplido con los correspondientes requisitos legales y reglamentarios.

Dado en Cuenca,

186

Exhibit 12

Actividades Desarrolladas

Regresar

No. Causa: 2012-0403

Judicatura: JUZGADO VIGESIMO CUARTO DE LO CIVIL

Acción/Delito: CONFESION JUDICIAL

Actor/Ofendido: PAEZ BENALCAZAR ANDRES TARQUINO

Demandado/Imputado: VINTIMILLA MOSCOSO MARIA XIMENA

Detalle de Actividades:

		Actividad
1	2012-04-16	COMPLETAR SOLICITUD Y/O DEMANDA

Previamente a calificar la demanda, el actor en el término de tres días, Precise contra quien dirige la petición, si en contra de la persona natural, o en contra de la Dra. María Ximena Vintimilla Moscoso en calidad de Jueza de la Corte Nacional. Notifíquese

Exhibit 13

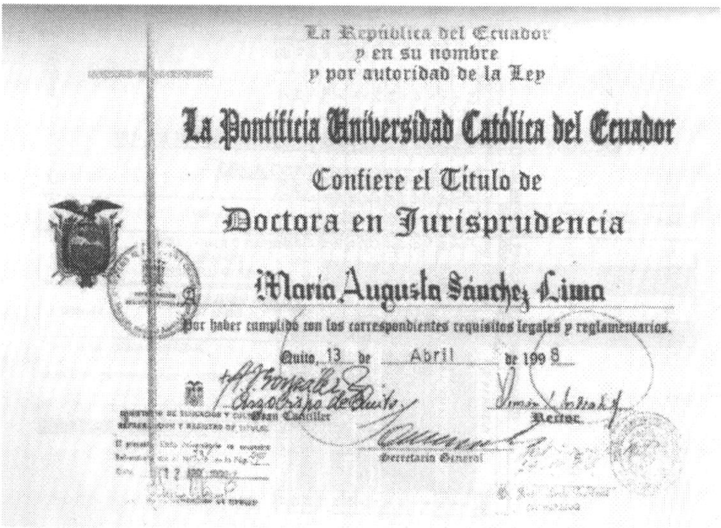
La República del Ecuador
y en su nombre
y por autoridad de la Ley

La Pontificia Universidad Católica del Ecuador

Confiere el Título de

Doctora en Jurisprudencia

María Augusta Sánchez Lima

Por haber cumplido con los correspondientes requisitos legales y reglamentarios.

Quito, 13 de Abril de 1998

Gran Canciller

Rector

Secretario General

Exhibit 14

CONCURSO JUECES Y JUEZAS CORTE NACIONAL DE JUSTICIA
RESULTADOS DEFINITIVOS

No.*	POSTULANTE	MERITOS	TEORICA	PRACTICA	SOBRE 90	AUDIENCIA	TOTAL
1	BERMUDEZ CORONEL OSCAR EDUARDO	30	27	26,1	83,1	6,9	90
2	RAMIREZ ROMERO CARLOS MIGUEL	27	27	27,09	81,09	9	90,09
3	MERCHAN LARREA MARIA ROSA	25	29,1	25,86	79,96	5	84,96
4	SUING NAGUA JOSE	28	24	27,75	79,75	7	86,75
5	ROBALINO VILLAFUERTE VICENTE	23	27,9	28,38	79,28	10	89,28
6	GRANIZO GAVIDIA ALFONSO ASDRUBAL	30	21,9	26,48	78,38	9	87,38
7	OJEDA HIDALGO ALVARO VINICIO	27	22,2	28,56	77,76	9,2	86,96
8	ESPINOZA VALDIVIEZO MARIA DEL	26	25,8	25,43	77,23	4,5	81,73
9	BLUM CARCELEN JORGE MAXIMILIANO	29	23,7	23,55	76,25	6	82,25
10	TERAN SIERRA GLADYS EDILMA	28	21,3	26,27	75,57	5	80,57
11	BENAVIDES BENALCAZAR MERCK	28,5	20,4	26,49	75,39	6	81,39
12	YUPANGUI CARRILLO YOLANDA DE LAS	33	15,6	26,79	75,39	1,33	76,72
13	MERINO SANCHEZ WILSON YOVANNY	27,5	21,9	25,11	74,51	7	81,51
14	FLORES MIER EDGAR WILFRIDO	27	22,8	24,3	74,1	1,2	75,3
15	PEREZ VALENCIA MARITZA TATIANA	28	23,1	22,68	73,78	8	81,78

Exhibit 15

PUNTAJE POR MERITOS PARA ELECCION DE JUECES Y JUEZAS
DE LA CORTE NACIONAL DE JUSTICIA

CEDULA	POSTULANTE	EXPERIENCIA LABORAL GENERAL PUNTOS	EXPERIENCIA LABORAL DEMOCRÁTICA EN PUNTOS	SEGURIDAD FORMAL ADICIONAL EN PUNTOS	CAPACITA CIÓN Y PUNTOS	CAPACITA CIONES IMPARTIDAS Y PUNTOS	PUBLICA CIONES IMPARTIDAS Y PUNTOS	ACCIONES AFIRMATIVAS 4 PUNTOS	TOTAL
020127836-3	YUMBAY YALLICO MARIANA 38 AÑOS (U. CENTRAL- MARZO 2001)	6	5	8	2	2	0	4	27
									21
171243584-6	SANCHEZ LIMA MARIA AUGUSTA 37 AÑOS (PUCE - ABRIL 1998)	10	1	4	1	1	0	4	21
									17

Fuente: www.funciónjudicial.gob.ec

Nota: Entre paréntesis, Fecha de Graduación que consta en el título profesional

	Puntaje asignado por méritos
	Puntaje asignado por méritos tomando en cuenta fecha de graduación

Exhibit 16

Exhibit 17

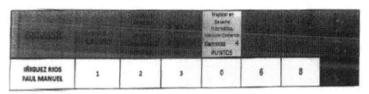

Art. 33.- Reglas para la calificación de méritos.- En la calificación de los méritos se observarán las siguientes reglas:

a) Para la asignación de puntajes en la calificación de educación formal adicional, no se considerarán los títulos por secuencia en diplomado, especialidad y maestría.

b) En los casos en que los certificados de capacitación recibida o impartida no incluyen explícitamente la información de la cantidad de horas impartidas, se asumirá como cinco (5) horas efectivas de capacitación recibido por cada día de asistencia reportado en el mismo certificado.

c) En el caso de artículos y ensayos, se adjuntará en formato electrónico, la información que demuestre que corresponde a una publicación indexada.

d) En el caso de libros, se adjuntará en formato electrónico la información de la publicación, en la que se haga constar el número de registro en el Instituto Ecuatoriano de Propiedad Intelectual.

e) Se verificará que la experiencia judicial, las obras jurídicas y las estudios especializados guarden relación con la especialidad de la Sala de la Corte Nacional de Justicia para la que postule.

Exhibit 18

PUNTAJE ELECCION DE JUECES Y JUEZAS
DE LA CORTE NACIONAL DE JUSTICIA

CEDULA	POSTULANTE	MERITO 30 PUNTOS	TEORICA 30 PUNTOS	PRACTICA 30 PUNTOS	TOTAL 90 PUNTOS	DIFERENCIA	AUDIENCIA 10 PUNTOS	TOTAL 100 PUNTOS	DIFERENCIA	PUESTO ANTES DE AUDIENCIA
170309415-9	YUPANGUI CARRILLO YOLANDA DE LAS MERCEDES	33	15,6	26,79	75,39	8.525	1,33	76,72	0,045	12
070227003-4	BLACIO PEREIRA LUCY ELENA	21	19,5	26,265	66,765		10,00	76,765		45

fuente: www.funcionjudicial.gob.ec

Exhibit 19

PUNTAJE POR MERITOS PARA ELECCION DE JUECES Y JUEZAS
DE LA CORTE NACIONAL DE JUSTICIA

CEDULA	POSTULANTE	EXPERIENCIA LABORAL GENERAL PUNTOS	EXPERIENCIA LABORAL ESPECIFICA 18 PUNTOS EL RAMA	EDUCACION FORMAL ADICIONAL 8 PUNTOS	CAPACITA CION 3 PUNTOS	CAPACITA CIONES COMPARTIDAS PUNTOS	PUBLICA CIONES 2 PUNTOS	ACCIONES AFIRMATIVAS 4 PUNTOR	TOTAL
0201271836-3	YUMBAY YALLICO MARIANA 38 AÑOS (U. CENTRAL- MARZO 2001)	6	5	8	2	2	0	4	27
		6		5	2	2		4	21
1712438884-8	SANCHEZ LIMA MARIA AUGUSTA 37 AÑOS (PUCE - ABRIL 1998)	10	1	4	1	1	0	4	21
		5		2	1	1		4	17

Fuente: www.funcionjudicial.gob.ec

Nota: Entre paréntesis, Fecha de Graduación que consta en el título profesional

	Puntaje asignado por méritos
	Puntaje asignado por méritos tomando en cuenta fecha de graduación

Exhibit 20

Consejo de la Judicatura

Oficio N° 259° DG-CJ-MP
Quito, 14 de septiembre de 2012

Señor Doctor
Andrés Páez Benalcázar
ASAMBLEÍSTA
En su despacho.-

De mi consideración:

En mi calidad de Director General y Representante Legal del Consejo de la Judicatura, según lo previsto en el artículo 280, inciso segundo del Código Orgánico de la Función Judicial, en contestación a su oficio N° 3136-APB-ID-12-MOZ, mediante el cual solicita información contenida en 15 puntos, relacionada con el segundo informe de Veeduría Internacional; al respecto, cúmpleme informarle sobre cada punto lo siguiente:

RECIBIDO
Fecha: 17/09/2012
Hora: 20:00
Firma: MERIZALDE
Nombre: JOSE MERIZALDE

PRESIDENCIA
CONSEJO DE LA JUDICATURA DE TRANSICIÓN
Diana Rodríguez
ASISTENTE ADMINISTRATIVA

FECHA: ... HORA: ...

Exhibit 21

Quito, 21 de octubre de 2011

Señor Ingeniero
Marco Polo García
DIRECTOR NACIONAL DE PERSONAL DEL CONSEJO DE LA JUDICATURA
Presente.-

Señor Director:

Sandra Patricia Morejón Llanos, María Patiova Guerra Guerra, Remigio Antonio Auquilla Lucero, Carlos Eduardo García Torres, Diego Alfre Zalamea León, miembros del Comité de Expertas y Expertos, designado para colaborar en el Concurso de Méritos y Oposición, Impugnación Ciudadana y Control Social para la Selección y Designación de Jueces y Juezas de la Corte Nacional de Justicia, en alcance a la comunicación de esta misma fecha y que se relaciona con la evaluación de los méritos de las personas postulantes en el concurso señalado, le comunicamos que al calificar la experiencia laboral general se resolvió valorar el ejercicio de la profesión de abogado, la judicatura o la docencia universitaria en ciencias jurídicas, de forma simultánea y acumulable, por ser complementarias las experiencias certificadas por los postulantes (relacionadas pero no iguales), y por identificar el tiempo de dedicación efectivo para inferir el grado de desarrollo de sus habilidades para ser jueza o juez de la Corte Nacional de Justicia.

Del señor Director. Atentamente,

MARÍA PATLOVA GUERRA G.
Universidad Central del Ecuador

SANDRA PATRICIA MOREJÓN LL.
Universidad de Especialidades Espíritu Santo

REMIGIO ANTONIO AUQUILLA L.
Universidad del Azuay

CARLOS EDUARDO GARCÍA TORRES
Universidad Técnica Particular de Loja

DIEGO ALFREDO ZALAMEA L.
Delegado por el Consejo de la Judicatura de Transición

CONSEJO DE LA JUDICATURA DE TRANSICIÓN
CERTIFICO QUE ES FIEL COPIA DEL ORIGINAL

Dr. Guillermo Falconí Aguirre
SECRETARIO GENERAL

Exhibit 22

Consejo de la Judicatura

Oficio N° 1842-DG-CJ-12-SEP
Quito, 20 de Julio de 2012

Señor Doctor
ANDRÉS PÁEZ BENALCAZAR
ASAMBLEÍSTA NACIONAL
En su despacho.-

De mi consideración:

En mi calidad de Director General y Representante Legal del Consejo de la Judicatura, según lo previsto en el artículo 280, inciso segundo, del Código Orgánico de la Función Judicial, en contestación a su oficio N° 2768-APB-ID-12-MOZ de 4 de julio 2012 mediante el cual solicita documentación certificada, cúmpleme informarle:

Exhibit 23

Quito, 21 de octubre de 2011

Señor ingeniero
Marco Polo García
DIRECTOR NACIONAL DE PERSONAL DEL CONSEJO DE LA JUDICATURA
Presente.-

Señor Director:

Sandra Patricia Morejón Llanos, María Patiova Guerra Guerra, Remigio Antonio Auquilla Lucero, Carlos Eduardo García Torres, Diago Alfre Zalamea León, miembros del Comité de Expertas y Expertos, designado para colaborar en el Concurso de Méritos y Oposición, Impugnación Ciudadana y Control Social para la Selección y Designación de Jueces y

Exhibit 24

REPÚBLICA DEL ECUADOR
ASAMBLEA NACIONAL

MEMORANDO No. SAN-2012- 1884

PARA: **ANDRES PAEZ**
Asambleísta

DE: **ANDRES SEGOVIA S.**
Secretario General

ASUNTO: En el texto

FECHA: Quito, 03 AGO 2012

En atención a su Oficio N° 2991-APB-ID-12-MOZ, me permito informar de acuerdo a los datos proporcionados por la página web del Concejo Nacional Electoral (http://app.cne.gob.ec/resultados2009/), y cuya copia adjunto, que el señor Rodrigo Collaguazo, es Asambleísta Suplente, electo para el Período Legislativo 2009 – 2013.

Exhibit 25

LA CORTE NACIONAL DE JUSTICIA

CONSIDERANDO:

Que el Informe Final presentado por la Veeduría Internacional a la Reforma de la Justicia en el Ecuador, "... *sugiere que la Corte Nacional de Justicia, como órgano máximo de la jurisdicción y a través de la Sala o del mecanismo que corresponda se pronuncie sobre la genuidad del proceso de selección de los jueces/zas de la misma producido; establezca las consecuencias del mismo; fije los parámetros en los cuales debe realizarse, y garantice el derecho al recurso en sede judicial del referido proceso a quienes resultaren preteridos(sic)*".

Exhibit 26

Correa's Invective: an Anthology

complex-ridden
rash-inducing
absurd scarecrow
gloom-and-doom prophets
20-square-block mayor
loan-sharking mayor
alcoholic
sourpuss
scandalmongers
amorphous
anachronistic
anarchists
girlie-like
babyish
opposed to progress
unethical
anti-country
unpatriotic
schemers
arrivistes
arrogant
human rights abusers
nonsense
trash
wild beasts
loud mouths
drunk
cretin
buzzard
buzzard-like speculators
golden bureaucracy
swindling bureaucracy
flying ass
fat-cheeked

unburied corpse
political corpses
riff raff
constipated-looking
mangy cartoonists
government-hater
idiot-face
Turk-face
toucan-face
last century's cave dweller
cave dwellers
charlatans
cheerleaders of neoliberalism
bonkers
gossipmongers
cynical
mischief-maker
sewer with antennas
coward
little pink plastic girls
sex-counseling virgins
coup plotters
corrupt
den of thieves
demagogues
masters in complaining
coup-plotting right
discredited
shameless
unhinged by greed
purveyors of misinformation
logbook of shame
absolutely mediocre leaders
masquerading as a journalist

masquerading behind an ink-
pot
double morality
drug addict
druggie
epitome of bad journalism
stateless businessmen
bragging dwarf
mini-Latin Lover
Mickey-Mouse pollster
sick
green with envy
speculators
swindler
swindlers
human stupidity
stupid
exploiters
fallacious
falsettos
braggart
farcical
black-shirted fascist
fascists
fundamentalists
scavengers
loan sharks
damaged people
lying people
horrid fat woman
big-time criminals
tight-assed li'l gringos
talkers
sons of the oligarchy
hypocrite
idiot
ignoramus
imbeciles

incapable
incapable of thought
incompetent
worthless
ineffable
vile
immoral
insignificant
mediocre investigators
irresponsible
silly left
chief of the Jurassic Park
his head won't take him any
farther
pubic louse
underhanded
thief
addlepated
rather limited
he was carrying a whole drug-
store on him
furious madmen
stuff of warriors, stuff of pick-
pockets
mafia
insolent brat
brats
bad faith
wife-beating mason
neighborhood tough guy
half man, half woman
mediocre
slandering mediocrities
long-haired
liars
mercenary woman
miserable
mythomaniac

cocktail-sipping mummies
unpleasant female
nefarious woman
narcopoliticians
can't walk and chew gum at
the same time
good-for-nothing bums
myth-makers
stubborn hater
labor oligarchy
opportunist
parapoliticians
poster boys
clowns
ne'er-do-well
ragamuffins
fat cat country
fat cats
never –growing midgets
loser
yellow rags
wicked journalist
semi-ignorant journalists
mad dogs
persecutor
scoundrels
smurf
grumpy smurf
poor man
rottenness
corrupt politician
two-bit politician or two-block
mayor
cheap two-bit politician
golden ponchos
crap
yellow press
corrupt press

corrupt international press
mean press
overbearing
pseudo-analysts
pseudo-businessmen
swine
rabble-rousers
king of the world
ridiculous
know-it-all
snitches
satraps
he thinks he's hot stuff
grave-digger
grave-diggers of education
rascal
sufferer
terrorists
has a shoe for a head
twerp
puppet
silly astrologer
fools
dumb
land-trafficker
traitor
bad-faith traitor
traitors to their country
troglodytes
big noses
usurer
sacred cows
seller of his own country
poisonous animals
party-system widow

Exhibit 27

PRESIDENCIA DE LA REPÚBLICA

Del escritorio de:

Dra. Pamela Martínez Loayza / Esp.

Asesora del Señor Presidente de la República

Rodrigo:

De acuerdo a lo conversado, acompaño la HV de Moisés Mieles, compañero que podrá ser de mucho beneficio para la Institución PM 5/I/2012

La comisión calificadora del concurso para integrar la Corte Constitucional en funciones estuvo presidida por Pamela Martínez Loayza, quien se desempeñó como asesora del presidente Correa y recomendaba a personas para que ocupen cargos públicos como el caso de Moisés Mieles, cuya contratación fue solicitada a Rodrigo Vélez, del CONSEP, mediante una esquela escrita con su puño y letra y con el membrete de la Presidencia de la República.

Fondo Editorial del IID

01. Cayetano Llobet: *Sendas de Libertad*
02. Alberto Valencia: *Historias de Guerra y de Paz en el Caguán*
03. Alexis Ortiz: *La política es chévere*
04. Guillermo Lousteau: *Democracia y Control de Constitucionalidad*
05. Carlos Alberto Montaner; *Latin American and the West*
06. Alberto Valencia: *"Cuando el éxito es un delito"*
07. Armando Valladares: *Contra toda esperanza*
0.8 Heriberto Justo Atuel: *"Política y Estrategia Internacional Contemporánea"*
09. Eduardo Duhalde: *"Argentina Aflame"*
10. Guillermo Lousteau: *The Philosophical Foundations of American Constitutionalism*
11. Joel Hirst: *The ALBA*
12. José Ignacio García Hamilton: *Cultural Legacies and the Challenge to Latin American Modernity*
14. Eleodoro Galindo Anze: *El legado maligno*
15. Nicolás Márquez: *"El impostor. Evo Morales de la Pachamama al narco-Estado"*
16. Carlos Alberto Montaner: *The Cubans*
17. Nicolás Márquez: *"El cuentero de Carondelet. Rafael Correa"*
18. Osvaldo Hurtado: *21st Century Dictatorships: The Ecuadorian Case*
19. Carlos Sánchez Berzaín: *La dictadura del siglo XXI en Bolivia*
20. Andrés Páez: *Messing with Justice*

Serie "Democracy Papers"

01. "Into the Abbys. Bolivia under Evo Morales and the MAS" (Douglas Farah)
02. "La democracia en América Latina" (Kevin Casas, Edmundo Jarquin, Guillermo Lousteau y Alvaro Vargas Llosa)
03. "Ecuador at Risk. Drugs, Thugs, Guerrilas and *The Citizen's Revolution*" (Douglas Farah and Glenn Simpson)
04. "El Rol del Poder Judicial en el sistema democrático" (Marianela Crognale, Nicolás Santos, María A. Cardoso, María Teresa Garrido y Jennifer Meléndez Ochoa)
5. "El Nuevo Constitucionalismo Latinoamericano" (Guillermo Lousteau, Ignacio Covarrubias, Xavier Reyes y Pedro Salazar)
06. "Utilización política de la Justicia" (Juan Manuel González y Patricia Tarre Mozer)
07. "La injerencia castrista en América Latina"
08. "Los derechos humanos bajo el socialismo del siglo XXI" (Guillermo Lousteau, Janisset Rivero, Hugo Achá, Jorge Zavala Egas, Asdrúbal Aguiar"
09. "Inside Argentina. La Campora - Back to the future" (Douglas Farah)
10. "Hacia un nuevo Contrato Social" (José Benegas, Fernando Iglesias, Pablo da Silveira, Alejandra Salinas, Guillermo Lousteau)

Made in the USA
Charleston, SC
22 May 2014